Into the Wilderness

SAMANTHA NAGEL

ISBN: 979-8-3303-7818-0
Published by Samantha Nagel
For information, contact:
mssamanthanagel@gmail.com or visit
www.samanthanagel.com

Cover design by Luisa Galstyan

To Elle Benson, the one who continues to help me come home to myself. Thank you for being my sister in all my evolutions.
I love you.

"The doors to the world of the wild Self are few but precious. If you have a deep scar, that is a door, if you have an old, old story, that is a door. If you love the sky and the water so much you almost cannot bear it, that is a door. If you yearn for a deeper life, a full life, a sane life, that is a door."

**— Clarissa Pinkola Estés,
Women Who Run With the Wolves**

"I found a rainbow, rainbow, baby. Trust me, I know life is scary. But just put those colors on, girl. You gotta learn to let go, put the past behind you. Trust me, I know, the ghosts will try to find you. But just put those colors on, girl. Come and paint the world with me tonight."

— Kesha, "Rainbow"

Table of Contents

Foreword by Ellen Gilbert

We are all born in captivity to a culture hell-bent on keeping us from our true nature.

Look around at the signs: the warm electric glow of your phone, the empty belonging of social media, the nutritionless calories of processed food.

The howl of the wild comes for us all, and most will ignore it to remain in false belonging. For those of us who heed the call, there comes a point where we simply must shake out our wolf's fur and dart into the woods - whether it's quitting a corporate job, leaving a relationship that reinforces gender norms, or sharing our tender art with the world.

As a coach, I most often see it in my clients around their early to mid-thirties, but every once in a while, a twenty-something early bloomer or a woman going through menopause knocks on my proverbial door. It's as though they wake up one day and realize they've been living someone else's life. They no longer want insta-perfection with airbrushed success: the marriage they were convinced to have, the career they were told would fulfill every need, or the empty promises of the fashion-beauty-diet industry. In this unprecedented age of social media, aren't we so aware of the billions of potential eyeballs viewing our every move that we transform our bodies, our lives, and our values to earn this hollow validation? It's big business getting us to hate ourselves so our "self-love" can be marketed back to us.

It's around this time my clients stumble upon Women Who Run With the Wolves by Clarissa Pinkola Estés, The Heroine's Journey by Maureen Murdock, or Wild by Cheryl Strayed. They might start dreaming of wolves as one woman did, begin honoring their menstrual cycle instead of abhorring it, or be invited to a moon circle by a friend. To answer the call is to descend into the woods. The rite of passage tends to be the big breaks with convention, the coming out to parents and partners as a wild woman, or the all-consuming need to dance barefoot around a fire under the full moon (IYKYK). And while we desire to be witnessed, validated, and held on our initiatory journey, the truth is it's often a lonely affair. It may be ironic that to find belonging in the world we have to take this pilgrimage alone. But self-belonging is the necessary first step on the path of finding our authentic community.

Because we'll use anything as a shield, a substitute, an excuse - our relationship with our mother, our work, our lover, our kids. We think if we can achieve the perfect relationships externally, the one with ourselves will just fall into place. But the opposite is true.

Imagine you are a wolf in a robot world. You were raised as a robot and always believed that you are a robot. So you raise robot children, marry a robot partner, find robot friends, and build a happy and fulfilling life… for a robot. To awaken to your wolf nature would be quite alarming! The stakes would be so high in your robot life, that it would be easier to continue pretending to be a robot than to be a wolf. (Even though being a wolf would be the most natural thing in the world.) But would you ever be able to go back to pretending to be a robot? Once you see your wolf tail in the mirror, it's nearly impossible to unsee it.

That's why self-belonging is most important - once the robot remembers she's a wolf, she can be a wolf because she belongs to herself first and foremost. And she can show up in her robot life as a wolf and see what happens because she has the courage to stand in her truth. And maybe some of the robots realize they're also wolves. Maybe they felt unsafe until she showed them the wolf ways. And those that want to stay robots can stay robots, but now she can also find her wolfpack. That's the power of unleashing your howl - you do it for yourself, but you end up finding your people.

I remember when I heard the howl. It came gradually, louder and louder in the night, until I couldn't ignore it anymore. I took baby steps to heed it - first leaving a toxic job, then moving across the country to the high desert of New Mexico. "Surely I'll find my people here," I thought. But when I went to locate a moon circle or women's group, there was nothing. A voice inside said, "If you create it, others will come." One of the greatest acts of self-belonging I've ever taken was starting that first online women's circle. Overnight we had 40 members, and by the end of my time in New Mexico, our group had grown to over 100 sisters strong. Other examples of answering the howl included starting a coaching business, coming out as bisexual at 32, and leaving social media earlier this year. May we all continue to trek deeper and deeper into the forest as we become more and more our true selves.

I was honored and delighted when Samantha asked me to write the foreword for this collection of essays. Sam was one of my first clients when I became a coach in New Mexico, and we embarked together on this work of rewilding. Now I am on a new path, becoming a therapist in Maryland, and I hope to continue to be a guide for folks on their journey back to their wild nature. Upon reading them, I realized - these aren't just essays - they're postcards from that brave wilderness.

So, dear reader, where are you on your journey? Have you caught sight of your own wolf tail in the mirror? Are you dreaming of running through the woods in the moonlight? Let this book be your map - the journey might not be simple or easy, but it is the most natural thing in the world. So put down the robot costume and the weight of false belonging, whether that's social media, a co-dependent relationship, or someone else's idea for your life, and back away slowly. Then turn and run full speed into the woods… We'll be waiting. Just follow the howls.

Ellen Gilbert works at the intersection of culture, community, spirituality and wellness. As a coach, she works with women to amplify their leadership and sovereignty. Ellen is currently a student at the University of Maryland, pursuing a master's degree in social work to become a therapist. She holds a master's in international development from The New School and is a certified coach and yoga teacher.

Acknowledgements

I am deeply grateful to all those who made this book possible.

Thank you to all the amazing contributors of this collection for their vulnerability: Alex Avila, Michelle Belmont, Caidyn Curry, Sara Saint-Hogan, Shyanne Martinez, Alex Mirabal, Michelle Renee, and Kayleen Schenk. Your courage, bravery, and love have made this book exist. Thank you for trusting me in this process.

Thank you to Ellen Gilbert for writing the foreword, Luisa Galstyan (@luisa_galstyan on Instagram) for the beautiful cover art,

and most of all, for you, the reader.

Thank you for holding space for us as we go through this transformation together.

Introduction

I birthed the idea of this collection at the end of 2023, a year in which I experienced healing, growth, love, and bountiful connection. My word of the year had been "belonging," and it was the word that became my North Star. When I was wondering whether I should do something, how I should make a hard decision, it was through the lens of belonging.

I largely attribute this moral touchstone to the fact that I had a very acute, and painful, sense of non-belonging when I was growing up, and then into my twenties after that. I turned to the work of Mia Birdsong, Ellen Gilbert, Clarissa Pinkola Estes, and Becca Piastrelli, all wonderful authors and creators whose work centers on the power of belonging.

The word sounds simple, and yet, as I'm sure the contributors of this book can tell you, the felt sense of the word is not. It is deep, it is fleeting, it is cavernous, it is elusive, it is mysterious, it is painful, it's hard work, it's beautiful, it's deeply spiritual and yet completely agnostic.

Belonging is about coming home to the world around us (seen and unseen) our communities, and ourselves. Belonging is about recognizing and re-becoming our true, wild and free selves.

All the pieces of art and truth are parts of our stories to belonging and re-wilding. All the contributors in this anthology are from, have lived, or currently live in the abundantly beautiful land of New

Mexico, the home to 23 Indian tribes located in New Mexico - nineteen Pueblos, three Apache tribes (the Fort Sill Apache Tribe, the Jicarilla Apache Nation and the Mescalero Apache Tribe), and the Navajo Nation. The nineteen Pueblos are comprised of the Pueblos of Acoma, Cochiti, Isleta, Jemez, Laguna, Nambe, Ohkay Owingeh, Picuris, Pojoaque, Sandia, San Felipe, San Ildefonso, Santa Ana, Santa Clara, Santo Domingo, Taos, Tesuque, Zuni and Zia.

When I began putting all the collections together, in the year 2024 (my word of the year is "vibrant," if you're curious), I began to walk the road of separation, the first stage in a rite of passage. My mother died on June 3, 2024. I was set to get married on July 27.

As you will begin to infer from some of my pieces, my relationship with my mother is what many describe as "complicated." In fact, this was a sentence I heard over and over again that summer when people found out what happened: "Wow, I'm so sorry. I know your relationship with her was… complicated." It was usually then followed by inane platitudes or just wildly inappropriate comments, including but not limited to:

- "Don't worry, she's always with you!" (Cue the threatening music - what if I don't want her to be with me at all times? Although she never did have healthy boundaries…)
- "God works in mysterious ways!" (Your brain works in a mysterious way, if you think this is appropriate to say.)

- "I feel like I failed your mom, and I'm to blame!" (This tickles me. Why do people think they should process this with me, of all people?)
- "You know what's crazy? I had a feeling she died!!" (Congrats!!! You were right!! Minus 10 points for telling me.)
- "I know EXACTLY how you feel!!! My grandmother/neighbor/dog/turtle died!" (Bonus points for the person who compared it to her two-year relationship ending.) (Also, this is almost always followed by them proceeding to trauma dump their grief on me.)
- "What HAPPENED?? Tell me everything!!" (Um no? I haven't seen you in ten years.)
- "I LOVED your mom!!" (Really? She never mentioned you.)
- "I LOVED your mom!!" (Really? I recall you actively disliking her.)
- "Only the good die young!!" (No explanation needed why this is bad.)
- "You know what they say! God takes his favorite children first." (Well, your god sounds almost as narcissistic as my mother.)
- "She loved you SO much!!" (Really? She didn't love me enough to not sexually, emotionally, and physically abuse me.)
- "I understand the grief and overwhelm and stress you must be feeling! I'm also

working/studying/moving/getting divorced/living." (Not the same!)

- And lastly: "You're still upset about this?"

After cultivating a life of belonging, in the weeks that followed that horrible day, my sturdy foundation cracked. Some people showed up, some people didn't. Some people showed up for a little, then left. Some people tried to show up but did such a hurtful job, I pushed them away. New or previous people appeared and stayed. New or previous people appeared, then left again. Relationships were made, deepened, strengthened, weakened, illuminated, shattered, mended, and altered.

A rite of passage is separated into three parts: the separation, the transformation, and the return. As I said, I was getting ready to marry my now husband, another rite of passage, only a month and a half after the news. (Who has been my rock, my mirror, my compassionate partner in joy and pain, my helper, and my honey. In a way, this happening so shortly before our marriage helped ease any doubt that could possibly exist, because of the full hearted and genuine way he showed up for me.) In other words, I was being pushed into separation, whether I liked it or not.

And separate, I did, but not only from people around me. I separated from my understanding of the world, myself, my mother, life, friendships, partnership, work, purpose, a regulated sleep schedule, my body, my routine, everything. My sense of belonging was shattered.

My sense of sovereignty, anger, justice, and self-respect was born in its place. I set boundaries that I would have never set, I voiced my feelings freely that I normally would keep quiet, I pushed back when people acted poorly, I said no to favors that shouldn't have been asked, I didn't answer texts I didn't want to answer.

In that state of passionate self-care, I completed a pivotal stage in the journey to mother myself well. My priorities became myself, my partner, my sister, and our dogs. My North Star became positioned to Sovereignty.

Sovereignty is another way to say: I became wild.

I once described my grief as a feral cat. I became a mamma bear. I understood the concept of "running the wolves" on a deeper level. In that period of raw, animalistic, primal, selfish, turbulence, when I felt separate, I found a belonging so fierce and true, I realized something crucial about belonging:

There is no such thing as belonging and not being wild.
You cannot truly belong and still be tamed.
You can not be tamed and still belong.

I hope that these stories and poems, allow you to see the messy, painful, tender, joyful, true and beautiful experience that is belonging.

I hope you free yourself along the way. Come howl at the moon with us and sharpen your claws on the riverbed stones when you're ready.

And remember: you belong.

In all your mistakes, imperfections, tears, smiles, glorious rage, and tender humanness, you belong.

Alex Avila

Alex Avila has spent time as a writer in both Los Angeles and New York City but now calls Albuquerque home. She is currently developing 'The Mrs. Rochesters: A Jane Eyre Story.'

On 'Monsters' by Claire Dederer

In the last few moments of the film *Hemingway and Gellhorn (2012),* we see and hear Martha Gellhorn, the famous 20th century war-correspondent and third wife of Earnest Hemingway, tell her editor over the phone, "Its Gellhorn. I've decided to go after all. Why? Because as usual The [New York] Times got it wrong again. All that drivel, that goddamn objectivity shit. I'm going to be on the next plane. No? Well, goddammit, I'll pay on my own dime. I can't wait for you to grow a pair of balls. You relax..." After hanging up she looks to the window.

"I'm not dead yet, you fuck," she says to the crow who, moments before, had been tapping on her window. I love that line. It was a callback to earlier in the film where we are told through the visual language of ravens, sepia tone, and Hemmingway compelling her to "get in the ring," that Hemmingway was the one who inspired her, with the pair constantly having a similar go at other writers of their time. Even if their love for one another did not survive; their love for the truth did. Gellhorn is mentioned in passing within *Monsters* by Clare Dederer. She would have wanted it that way. She never wanted to be known as 'Hemmingway's wife.' It's hard to know if she got her wish. In war correspondence circles, she was a force of her own, a hurricane. She was the first reporter on the beaches of Normandy on D-Day, smuggling herself onto one of the ships in a nurses uniform. In literary fiction circles, she is known as the only woman who left Hemmingway. Life and influence are about perspective. Hemingway is mentioned in Dederer's text extensively, both in his genius and flawed humanity. According to Dederer, the writer Martha Gellhorn didn't think the artist needed to be a monster; she thought the monster needed to make himself into an artist.

"A man must be a very great genius to make up for being such a loathsome human being."[1] Many monstrous men are loathsome human beings. Women are as well, though not enough for Claire Dederer or my own liking. (See her chapter on *Abandoning Mothers*). Few women have been given the license to act monstrously in society outside of cautionary fairy tales. It is one of the things Dederer makes us wonder about in her book. Where are our feminine monsters? Why are there not more? What is the perspective we may be putting someone into where they either do or don't belong? *Monsters* is a work about feeling - what we feel, why we feel, and how we feel. To approach society's creative monsters with logic implies a "moral calculator," to use Dederer's words, when there isn't, or at least not one fine-tuned enough to consider every experience. What we feel becomes legitimized on her pages, becoming its own sort of individual theology.

Religiously speaking, feelings operate in a strange way, as does perspective. We are meant and encouraged to trust lofty feelings, feelings that get us out of our body, almost like floating. Things like serenity, which I discovered the author Joan Didion always associated with death, are encouraged. It's something that removes us from control of our feelings and can be encouraged as well. Depending on the church, one is allowed to be moved by the Holy Spirit, within reason. Speaking in tongues is also allowed. Demonic possession though had to be rid of because that was the wrong surrendering. Whether one invited these demons is up for theological debate. Passion for the Lord was alright; passion for a boy had to be resisted (ironic considering our Lord Himself became a human as the Christ figure, craving the subjectivity of existence despite living a completely objective one, per the Christian myth). Disgust for humans is discouraged, but disgust for the dreadful things humans did is encouraged. It felt like there was no way to be a human without keeping the score or without wondering if one had let themselves get too far ahead. There are right feelings to be had and wrong ones. So, we try to be stoic, yet without much success, considering we are not able to weigh life correctly or be objective enough. This is something we feel instinctually, especially when we are tasked with trying to vilify or nullify the 'monsters' of the world and the art we make. What's love got to do with it? Everything.

[1] Dederer, Claire. *Monsters: A Fan's Dilemma*. 1st

ed., *Penguin Random House*, 2023. p. 174.

That is what I thought of whilst reading *Monsters* by Claire Dederer, which has easily become nestled into my top ten favorite books of 2023. Validation of perspective is the gift of Dederer. Getting rid of the 'objectivity shit.' Because that's what it is: bullshit. We mock ourselves by pretending that our own lives are not the baggage we bring to art. To use a word that Dederer uses herself, the actions of artists do 'stain' their art. Give yourself permission to take weeks with this book, make notes, watch *Midnight in Paris (2011)*, let yourself be disappointed, and let yourself be lifted up as well. Be moved and be immovable. The tension of being human is learning how to live in the spaces between – between a million things, between you and the world, between you and whatever deity calls your soul, between the questions and the answers. Of course, questions are more important than the answers and to quote Andrea Long Chu when she was featured on the podcast *High Low with EmRata*, "It is the critic's job to tell people how to think, not what to think." Dederer is telling us not only how to think, but giving us permission to tell others. Feeling is the body's way of thinking and weighing; it is how we live. You cannot live someone else's life for them, Barbie's *Princess and the Pauper (2004)* notwithstanding. You can also not love someone else's passion for them. You cannot clean out a stain of someone that you did not create, nor is on your own clothes. We must forgive one another, though not necessarily these people, even if their crimes did not happen to us, but we must forgive one another for our problematic favorites. If we cannot forgive one another then the monsters win because their stain will then spread to the ones we love and respect. We will equate the appreciation of *Annie Hall (1977)* with approval of emotionally grooming one's girlfriend's daughter, which I doubt any of us are secretly aching to do. The truth is that these men have made things which made us feel human, seen, and understood as well as accepted. It frightens us to identify ourselves with them at all, but just because we see that the monster has eyes like ours doesn't mean that we now have horns. To paraphrase the brilliant Azar Nafisi, to understand doesn't mean that we condone. Would it not be as important to understand where the monsters came from? As uncomfortable as it is, there is less separating the monsters from us. At the same time, others would ask me to juggle. Is it incumbent on us to understand them? Victims are often, repeatedly, being asked to be understood, while we 'understand' monsters without little forethought or stress. They are begging to be considered. Selfishness of the artist is given space to breathe as well. Working mothers and women may not be monsters as we think of them, but there is an inherent selfishness to the notion of making art and being asked to be alone with that art. All these concerns are brilliantly articulated and given space by

Claire Dederer. She balances and considers in ways that will quiet even the most pedantic "well, actually" observer from the crowd.

As I write this, a picture of my mother and myself stares at me from my writing desk. I wonder how much of this my own mother felt. She was a writer, editor, and translator. I wonder how monstrous she allowed herself to be. Perhaps too much, perhaps not enough. Is the answer to all of this in *Monsters*?

"What do we do about the terrible people in our lives? Mostly we keep loving them…When I was young I believed in the perfectibility of humans. I believed that the people I loved should be perfect and I should be perfect too. That's noy quite how love works."[2]In the end, the answer is unsatisfying because life is unsatisfying. Why do we love these works and these men? Because we love them; we love them both, like the neglected child who loves his mother even after years of therapy. Like the scorned and thrown-about wife or like the boyfriend who never told us they loved us. We love them anyway. Love is not rational or something that can be ushered away with facts. It is love. It makes us hypocrites. It makes us interested. It makes us human.

[2] Dederer, Claire. *Monsters: A Fan's Dilemma*. 1st ed., *Penguin Random House*, 2023. p. 256.

THE CRITIC AND SHERLOCK HOLMES

"I am a brain, Watson. The rest of me is a mere appendix."

- Sherlock Holmes, The Adventure of the Blue Carbuncle (1892)

As a teenager I became obsessed with Sherlock Holmes. Not only because I adored Guy Ritchie's film adaptation and read the stories, but also because I was a teenage girl. On the trip to Sweden after the death of my mother, I read a book with a red cover that was about the fighting styles and truths of the time that Sherlock Holmes was set in. I first was introduced to the character when I was ten years old when Robert Downey Jr. portrayed him on the screen, then again at twelve years old with the books, and then thirteen with the BBC miniseries. I was late to the party to say the least; he had been around since 1887. Sherlock Holmes was a fictional creation of Sir Arthur Conan Doyle, a man with a genius mind, a drug addiction, a predilection for the violin, and a nose for solving crime. The books and short stories are from the point of view of his companion and crime-solving colleague, Dr. Watson. He accompanies his friend and flatmate on various cases wherein Sherlock acts as a "consulting detective." From the smallest scuff on a shoe or a loose thread on a shirt, he would be able to conclude where someone was from, their profession, and a myriad of other details. He is a perfect detective, but an imperfect man. He is not known for being interested in relationships of any kind and being emotionally abusive at times to those around him. He is also known for being a severe drug addict. He solves crimes involving everything from simple theft, to hunting down leaked pornography for royalty, to uncovering human trafficking rings. He is one of the best characters in fiction to ever exist. He has been adapted into probably half a million times into shows, films, graphic novels, animes, short stories, and at least 10,000 fanfictions on Archive of Our Own (AO3). We will be looking at one of these adaptations: the BBC series starring Martin Freeman as Dr. Watson and Benedict Cumberbatch as Sherlock Holmes.

It is Sherlock Holmes in the modern day. He loves smartphones and quips. You can look up "Sherlock insulting people " on YouTube and get hundreds of hits. It is not the purest expression of the character, but we will be using the portrayal of Sherlock Holmes in the show *Sherlock (2010)* for this essay, for several reasons.

Reason One: it made me fall in love with intellectual men in dark suits.

Reason Two: it made my 13-year-old brain fall in love with Sherlock Holmes.

Reason Three: it puts Sherlock Holmes into the modern day.

Reason Four: I have spent more time with the show than I have with the books and short stories, something that in the end, I think that Sir Arthur Conan Doyle would appreciate.

I think I know the reason I was so drawn towards

Sherlock. I think I know the reason why teenagers were drawn to the BBC series and loved the characters so much. In a place where the world doesn't make sense and adults don't make sense, here is an adult who understands. He may not understand how feelings or love work practically, but we do not need him for that. I have never met a teenage girl who was not willing and able to give herself over to love right away (to be fair, most of the teenagers I knew when I was a teenager were theater kids and theater kids possess highly intense feelings). Sherlock Holmes may not care or understand about paying bills or feelings, but he understands things other people do not. He himself is a teenager – someone who is specialized, but not necessarily adept toward the things he should be. He feels like a good counterpart. He is bitchy and mean. He is unreasonable. He makes enemies. Sometimes he makes enemies from doing good, solving crimes, and unearthing black market art rings. Often, he makes enemies by pointing out when people are having affairs, have gained weight, or when they are wearing lipstick to "compensate" for their ugliness – again, like a teenager. Another good counterpart to the American teenager is the Critic.

Critics are usually the villains within art house movies. They are the people who are paid to have an opinion, though more often than not, they are not paid. Critics are detectives. You may watch a movie and not be able to pinpoint why the movie is no good, but the

Critic knows. They can know when the pacing is off, that the characters are not fleshed out, or the script was generally terrible. They are pattern identifiers. They notice everything. Critics and Sherlock Holmes notice things. There is one mystery that Sherlock has to solve wherein he has to prove that a painting within a gallery is a fake. He is able to prove its inauthenticity because there is a constellation featured in the starry backdrop of the painting that would not have been discovered or observed by astronomers until years after the painting was manifested. Critics are meant to view the minutia within a piece of art. They both take a certain pleasure in the hunt. Sherlock will not take any cases that do not interest him because it is a waste of his time. We see a revolving door of clients who do not interest him because their cases are too simple. There is no hunt in the hiker who returned from foreign travel and then ended up dead after a car backfired. But the geeks who interpret comics only to have the comic come true or a cluster of individual suicides that despair different backgrounds, mental states, ages, races, gender, and status? These are all interesting and require unpacking. They

require explanation. The "nepo baby" who thinks he can create a film with no vision? Boring. The writer who seems to pathologically pick gay men to write about and put them through a circus of trauma for her narrative fulfillment? That is more engaging.

With an almost pathological inability to purely enjoy anything, the Critic is accused of being unable to find pleasure, the same way that we see that Sherlock is unable to relax. Whenever he doesn't have a case, he has a propensity to dive into drug use. That is the cry against the Critic by the masses, "It's not that deep!" "Why can't you just let people like something?" It is less about not letting people like something and more about noticing the problems. True, no one wants to be the person who notices problems everywhere, but not everyone is the Critic, or Sherlock.

The Critic and Sherlock do have something they like. The most intense joy comes from making a discovery, making connections between seemingly unrelated things. It is the main joy of my critical essays and it is the joy of Sherlock's. The giddy way that he explains a murder or a discovery. We all miss the small things and miss one another every single day and it is the joy of people like Sherlock and the Critic to make the connections. It is their gift to us as well.

The Critic and Sherlock thrive in a community even if they do not always fit into this community. Sherlock is nothing without Watson, Mycroft, Molly, Inspector Lestrade, Mrs. Hudson, or the hundreds of other people who he employs – not to mention his underground "Baker Street Irregulars," a network of homeless individuals whom he pays to be his eyes and ears on the street whenever he's investigating. Sherlock would never be able to survive without crime and crimes only happen where there is community.

The Critic could never survive without community as well. What is the point in discovering beautiful things when there is no one to tell you about it? What is the point of discovering a murderer if there is no justice? My personal favorite critic, Andrea Long Chu, speaks of how criticism is like flirting. Flirting isn't to prove to someone you like them, it's to give them the opportunity to show that they like you. The deduction isn't to prove that Sherlock is smart and understands, we already know, for better or for worse, that he understands and is smart. It's to show us that we can understand and to explain things to us. The way that Sherlock describes and explains everything to everyone, it feels like a dance, almost a seduction. That's why in season two of *Sherlock*, when Irene Adler explains how a certain hiker died, he is both in awe and swept up in her. His deduction is seduction. As much as we may hate critics, and as much as those within his universe hate Sherlock, perhaps we need them both. Not all the time, hopefully, but whenever we need to be taught how to think, how to notice, and how to ruffle feathers, there they are.

IS IT OVER NOW?

When does a relationship actually end? When is someone actually gone? According to Taylor Swift, Lissa Soep, and Mikhal Bakhtin, the answer is more complicated than anything we might configure. Let's dive into Taylor Swift first because I could not help but obsessively listen to her songs "from the Vault," especially those from 1989. I listened to *Now That We Don't Talk* on a loop for five hours while wandering through the Houston Fine Arts Museum – which I would highly recommend. *Is It Over Now?* came on while I was driving to work, and it made me cry in a way I did not expect. It made me think of a book I had just finished. It reminded me of two good friends who I do not speak to and will probably never speak to again. It reminded me of my mother.

> *"Was it over when she laid down on your couch?*
> *Was it over when he unbuttoned my blouse?*
> *"Come here," I whispered in your ear.*
> *In your dream as you passed out, baby.*
> *Was it over then? And is it over now?"*

The plea to know when something was over; that's what the song is about. Taylor Swift understood something I had never been able to articulate which is relationships were not over the second that two people decided to not be in one another's lives. I dove into the lyrics. Sure, my loves were not necessarily about the loss of a British popstar's love, but it was still loss. I wondered if the relationships were over for good, if there were parts of them that lived on.

Other People's Words is a book about grief by Lissa Soep. She writes about the deaths of two very good friends, one over time and one immediately. She understands. *Other People's Words* takes its title from a Russian philosopher – stay with me. The quote, "For the prose artist the world is full of other people's words, among which he must orient himself and whose speech characteristics he must be able to perceive with a very keen ear. He must introduce them into the plane of his own discourse, but in such a way that this plane is not destroyed." In short, the people who interact with us, their words are woven into our own. Soep effortlessly weaves the concepts of Bakhtin into the journey of her own grief. A journey that makes her, and me as the reader, realize the cliche is true: those we love are not truly gone. A literary critic and philosopher of the turn of the century, Bakhtin was interested in the communal nature of not only art, but our own existence. No life is untouched by another. Originality is a myth. The pleasure of existence is meeting amazing people whose virtues and vices become our own – and that a relationship never truly ends because we picked up parts of them in ourselves. This is both a frustration and a comfort to me as a writer for I pride myself on the particularities of my words, and as a human, for there are people I have loved who I wish I could forget. Lissa Soep, a PhD recipient from Stanford, lost a close friend to dementia and another one to a boating accident: Christine and Jonnie. Grief aches and stings. Christine and her partner Mercy were part of an intense friend quartet that included Soep and her husband. Mercy left Christine around the beginning signs of dementia, though no one knew it was dementia at the time. All they knew, and Mercy knew, was that Christine was not herself anymore and she was changing. Mercy carries complicated guilt as her former lover harasses her with emails, letters, and phone calls. Mercy's silence tortures Christine even as her brain starts to fade and the parts of her that everyone loved become lost. Jonnie dies in a boating accident leaving behind a family who mourns the loss intensely. Traditions are carried on in the name of the loved ones that were lost. Years later Jonnie and his wife Emily's child Max has a B'nai Mitzvah. At the reception, after Emily repeats an affirmation that Soep remembers Jonnie telling Emily when she was pregnant with Max. "Shake it, Mama!" History can repeat in a wonderful way, like a hiccup, unexpected and disrupting the motions one was just going through. In my experience, it can be as unpleasant as a hiccup to remember something or someone. That you tilted your wrist in the way they did when they were disregarding your pain during a fight. You jutted your chin out the way they used to when you confronted them. When are things over?

Through the woven threads of us all, there is no way of truly knowing how connected we all are or where your life touches another. Bakhtin himself has been credited as the "true author" of many texts that never bore his name. His idea that the imagination and the creative muse were never things that one person owned. Some of these texts he could have written, but there were other texts he did not contribute to. What injured parts of me were written by someone else – written by someone else, but I credited myself as the sole author of the pain? I thought of the friends who excommunicated themselves from my lives, friends who I had late night drinks with, friends who knew every desire I had ever had. Friends who were my confessors and who confessed to me as well in turn. Friendships that had no office hours. I wonder at those who have hurt me. I wonder if they know about the colors that have been woven into me. What parts can I not cut out without unraveling the whole thing? I am not grateful for the pain given to me by them, but I know that my life, the tapestry, would not be the same without it. It is holding together parts of my story. As much as I want to leave them behind, I cannot. As much as that is frustrating, I also know this: I am a part of their story. They can deny it. They can try to cut me out, but they cannot truly cut me out. They could never think of me again, but I would still be a part of their story. I would still be woven in. I matter to the grand story of history, even if they did not think I mattered in even a little of their times. The pain of that stings, but not as much as it stung to think that I had never affected them. I did.

At the end of the book Mercy goes into the boxes that Christine left for her, eight years after Christine died. Amazing signs of her life: a picture of their shared cat, a birthday card, a ski pass from when Christine was young. Even her own birth certificate. Pocket litter, postcards, papers – the signs of a life that was lived. Things that say "I was here. I was a present tense once. I wasn't always the past." A handwritten love note from before they broke up, thought to be lost in a great fire Christine lit to burn all of Mercy's letters. In the same way that Christine's words were coming back to Mercy, Mercy's words had never really left Christine. Signs of their love. It was almost like Christine had come back to them. I recognized this sensation. The moment I discovered the perfume that my mother wore, Bvlgari Omnia, when a stranger passed by me, or reading *Anne of Green Gables* while driving through the Swedish countryside for her funeral. The book she loved, the country she loved, it was like she was there, holding my hand. The older I get, the more my hands look like hers, a mole appearing on my right hand where she used to have one. I never remembered it appearing, but my hands look like hers now. The painting that a family-friend did of her, the image of her in a white shirt and the background was the lake near our home, made her look like a goddess. She loved a soy-chai from Starbucks and the taste of one makes me think of her. It felt like a part of her came back. It felt like maybe for the rest of my life, parts of her would keep coming back. I loved that. The love I had and have for my mother continues, complicated and wonderful. My mother might be lost to me, but she keeps being found as well.

SALTBURN ESSAY

If we get up for ourselves, we live for pleasure, interest or boredom (the aesthetic life). If we get up for others, we live according to universal moral principles (the ethical life). Finally, if we get up for God, then we live for an absolute power that creates and supports us (the religious life)- Soren Kierkegaard

What this movie isn't: a story of eat the rich. It is not a story of the rich being devoured by someone who isn't their own. This is a love story and a story of aesthetic life. It could also be the story of devotion to a human being, to love. A love story wherein the memory of someone that is imbued with a place must be devoured. A story of possession, which is the only way a flawed love by flawed people can manifest. When a person is a place, you must have that place to experience them. It is why Heathcliff must have Wuthering Heights.

This is not going to be a story about ethics, or merit the way other Oxford stories are.

The character of Michael who is 'reading' (studying- the US equivalent) maths proclaims himself a genius. This genius status is not treated the way it is in other genius narratives. In movies that show the humbling genius, their genius is shown as something that differentiates them from others but also helps them find their own people and save others. Think of Oppenheimer or The Imitation Game wherein intelligence is seen over time as a virtue. While here Micheal is shown as a nuisance. He is not given any other redeeming character traits. He has a superiority complex, he is rude, he is domineering, and he is seen as a force that will keep Oliver away from Felix.

Oliver reveals to his tutor that he did the entire reading list, which was about 50 books. His tutor is incredulous, saying that even he himself has not read all the books. There is a general attitude of 'don't try so hard.' There is disdain for Oliver as he is seen wearing the school jacket. His reading aloud of his essay is of no interest to his tutor. Oliver has no 'place' to link his personhood the way Farleigh and Felix do. He comes from no long history.

He is architecturally anonymous.

Think of the main character, Edmund Dantes, in 'The Count of Monte Cristo'- no one quite trusts this Count because no one knows where Monte Cristo is but as a wealthy mannered landed mysterious person he is allowed access to society. Oliver is given no such leeway because he has no money, no knowledge of how life goes on in these buildings, and no place of his own.

The message: if you have to prove that you belong here, you don't belong here. We as the audience belong here because we
are seeing it, we are being taken along for the ride. We belong here. So let's dive in.
This story will be about knowledge, but about how you know people. How you know about what belongs to them. This is a world wherein how things look matters. (Evidenced by Felix's mother Elsbeth stating how she cannot stand ugliness, how it repels her. Thank god her children are good looking.) These people do not need uniforms to show they belong amongst the architecture, they

come from families that know they belong. They have nothing to prove. Their lines are as ancient as the architecture. Architecture and personhood, like many medieval stories, are linked together. Look at Wuthering Heights by Emily Bronte, The Hunchback of Notre Dame by Victor Hugo and so many others. People are linked to places within these narratives and unable to escape them. Felix is Saltburn, and that is why Oliver must have it.

Oliver might seem like a symbol of the ethical life, what with the story of his rising out of poverty he tells Felix, but in fact he is for the aesthetic life.

'You are picking apart the style of my essay rather than the substance.' This is what Oliver says to Farleigh, and this is the thesis of the wealthy world where Farleigh and Felix come from. How does it look?

The price for how something looks is always the truth of what it is. The phrase, 'it's not a good look,' means that regardless of the truth of something it matters how it appears. It is how Oliver is able to get away with his actions. It doesn't matter that Farleigh did not send the email threatening to sell memorabilia of Saltburn to an auction house- it looks like he did.

These people are not interested in the truth, and Oliver says as much when he confronts Felix at the garden party saying to Felix that the story Oliver told him is what he wanted. That he was being like everyone else, giving Felix what he wanted.

In the same way that these wealthy lives were organized by deceit, and taking advantage of others- Oliver also takes advantage of those around him to get what he wants. He proves he is willing to pay the price for the aesthetic life.

SAMANTHA NAGEL

WE HAVE ALWAYS LIVED IN THE MANSION

"There's a lot of baggage that comes with us, but it's like Louis Vuitton

baggage; you always want it."

- Kim Kardashian

"Where would we go?" she replies. "What place would be better for us

than this? Who wants us, outside?

The world is full of terrible people."

- We Have Always Lived in the Castle (1962)

I have never watched more than an episode or two of *The Kardashians (2022)* and I probably never will. I cannot even tell you what the episode was about, nor can I tell any of the sisters apart. At the same time, I know so much about them. Their influence as a family has ranged from courtrooms to reality television, to healthcare and now to law itself as Kim Kardashian studies to become a lawyer. One could avoid any tabloid magazines or social media and still be affected by their divorces and brand deals. Who is this family? Touted as everything from the second coming of Jezebel to misunderstood, feminist icons, the Kardashian women read as the definitive novelistic figures. Think of Cathy from *Wuthering Heights (1847)*: bratty, sullen, and disagreeable. Think of Becky Sharp who constantly vies for an advantageous marriage, not caring who she might be leaving behind. Numerous "difficult" women exist in the pages of books that we devour as voraciously as any magazine or Instagram reel. Think of Daisy Buchanan, floating on her money and influence even as dead bodies pile around her – even ones she passively piled, with her lover amongst them. I tell you though, the sisters that the Kardashian family reminds me the most of is not the Bennets, though many have compared the family matriarch, Kris, to Mrs. Bennet. It is the Blackwood sisters from Shirley Jackson's *We Have Always Lived in the Castle (1962)*.

Much like a female, Greek monster or a goddess born from the sea, this family does have an origin. Despite their mythical proportions; however, they are not mythological. They are human. So human that they have made their wealth off things that the American public is fascinated with, such as sports, murder, and sex. Their family has been reality television royalty since 1995, when Rob Kardashian defended OJ Simpson in his murder trial. The second eldest of the Kardashian girls, Kim, became a stylist to many celebrities of the aughts. Though her essential rise to fame arose when she starred in a sex tape (though "starred" implies that she consented to it being released, which she did not and for which she sued her costar for releasing, but we are not focusing on him.) When the tape premiered in February of 2007, her mother used this as a jumping-off point for the Kardashian reality show *Keeping up with the Kardashians.* It premiered in October of that same year. The Kardashians' sins have been documented for almost 20 years now – their ups and downs. They have their lovers and haters alike. We cannot escape them. They are women, and a few men, that most everyone will have an opinion on, much like the Blackwell women in Jackson's novel. Many people are only familiar with Shirley Jackson in the vein that they were forced to read her incendiary short story *The Lottery (1948)* in school. Her works have been adapted to radio, television, and film. The most famous amongst them being *The Haunting of Hill House* for Netflix in 2018. Her life was also the inspiration for the film *Shirley (2020)*, a horror film I cannot recommend enough. My favorite of her works however must be *Hangsaman (1951)* about a young student who finds herself pregnant and goes missing.

Why am I reminded of Shirley Jackson when thinking of the Kardashians? Shirley Jackson knew better than anyone how women were watched, judged, and weighed. She herself was a female academic and a genius during a time when a woman was only expected to be married to a genius. She was also pulled into an open marriage, one that she did not want, but resigned herself to (not to be seen as a functioning example for non-monogamy). She herself was "othered" for these things, a theme that often permeates Jackson's other works. Women being othered, either by their own actions, their personalities, or their own inclinations. Jackson is concerned with how women are being perceived, hated, and adored. *We Have Always Lived in the Castle* was recently adapted to film in 2018 with lukewarm results despite excellent casting, sets, and director. For those who haven't read or watched, let me summarize.

The Blackwoods live on the edge of a village in a house called "The Castle." The blackwood family includes Uncle Julian, Constance the eldest sister, and our narrator Merricat. Merricat's eldest sister, Constance, has recently been acquitted of the charge of murder via poisoning the family. The poison was put in the sugar and the family put sugar on their berries. Constance was the only one to not put sugar on the berries and Merricat was sent to bed without dinner – four people killed, their parents included, and Uncle Julian injured. Charles comes to the house, a cousin of the girls, and starts to woo Constance. Merricat is suspicious, but as a practitioner of what is known as "sympathetic magic" she protects the home by burying valuable objects along the perimeter of the home. She tries to drive Charles away with this magic, but after accidentally starting a fire, we discover that Merricat was

the one who poisoned the family to stop the implied abuse of her father on her sister. During the fire, the people within the town loot and destroy most of the home. They are only satiated when Uncle Julian is found dead. The girls hide away from their cousin and the villagers who have left food on the doorstep of the remains of the house to atone. Merricat and Constance vow to live in the remains of the house and stay together. The book concludes with Merricat smiling for the first time in the whole of the book. What does a 20th century family, driven by fame and fortune, have in common with the Blackwood girls? Everything. The Blackwood girls are accused of being difficult, antisocial, and unproductive members of the village. Much in the same way that, especially during the Bush administration, the Kardashian family was accused of being everything that was wrong with American life – both being groups of women (though while the Kardashian family does include men, it is wildly confirmed to be a matriarchy with Kris Jenner as its overlord). Within social groups, we need and want to have someone to blame. In the absence of any religious enemies within the public, we turn to our celebrities and turn them into secular saints and demons. They want to be able to point to a group, usually marginalized, and say, "Look here! Aren't they awful?" From the Salem Witch Trials of Massachusetts to Donald J. Trump claiming that Jewish people control the media, we love to point the finger and claim something, or someone, is poisoning us.

Murder and sex are the two American pastimes with which we are fascinated. The first murder trial of the United States,[1] *People vs. Levi Weekes,* might well have been one of passion wherein a Mr. Weeks was accused of murdering the woman he was courting after she told a confidant that the pair of them were to elope. Murder is what propelled the Kardashians into the public, as well as Kim's sexuality. They became the perfect symbol of what we love to hate. Merricat's poisoning of her family to stop the abuse and Constance's taking the blame is something that those in the village gossip about constantly. Sure, both families had notoriety, but only fame and scorn came after. It wasn't just that Rob Kardashian was defending someone; he was defending one of the most famous athletes in America who killed his own wife. It wasn't just that the Blackwood patriarch died; it was that someone in his family killed him. The notion that someone under his own roof would have hated him as much as the villagers did for being rich and stingy was incendiary. We do not want to acknowledge the likeliness of being killed by someone who we are close to. We may not like them, but both groups give us something to talk about. The United States also loves gossip, something we most likely inherited from our British big siblings. Crime and fame function similarly within both groups of these women's lives. Both create distance from the normal experience of life as most people will not be famous. "Normal" people hate, love, and despair like famous people do, so we love to watch them struggle. We want them to be punished for their prosperity, but not fatally. The Kardashians when they go through a truly horrendous life event then they are surrounded with public cries for empathy or silence. Whether it's divorces, child-rearing troubles, cheating scandals, or even the bickering between siblings; we can see ourselves in them and condemn them all at once. Our ability to feel empathy for these people who could never or will never care about us makes us feel better about ourselves. At the same time, when we criticize them, we can be judge and jury all in one. You may not watch her show, but who has not enjoyed that little jolt of watching a television reel wherein we see Kim Kardashian unable to bond with her daughters or understand them? The villagers are willing to trash the castle and only when Uncle Julian dies do they withdraw. They do not want to become as "bad" as the Blackwells because then they cannot feel superior to them. After the death of Uncle Julian, the girls withdraw further into themselves, living in the one wing of the house that was not destroyed. and the villagers bring them food that is left on their doorstep. The true result of this vitriol, then kindness, then scorn, then worship means one thing about both these families: they turn into myth. The Kardashians are further revered and admired for the things they survive. The laying bare of their personhood draws us back. Their wealth and influence push us away. The Blackwell girls in their isolation become even more mythologized as they almost become like the witches that live in the forest. Mystery surrounds them yet again.

Shirley Jackson understood the struggles of being a woman that operates outside the standards of expected behavior for women. To be sure, murder and the release of a sex tape are very different things.

Merricat's wanting to end the implied abuse of her sister Constance is seen as a noble endeavor by the readers, we at least understand. The intimate relationship and the celebration of her body and sexuality can be seen as both a liberation and a classless action. However, what happened to Kim in 2007 would now be classified as a crime because she did not consent to the tape's release. This has now become commonplace unfortunately for famous women. Every few years there are phone hacks, data breaches, and outright theft, thinking of the Pamela Anderson sex tape, wherein women must publicly pay for the audacity of their sexuality and ongoing intimacy with men. Women's intentions to share something intimate with a partner now have become a public item to comment on. Merricat's private action meant to protect her sister from their parents, but then becomes public as Constance goes to prison and the village becomes obsessed with the Blackwoods. Murder and sex: two things we cannot get enough of in the United states. How

[1] "People v. Levi Weeks, 1800." Historical Society of the New York Courts, 9 Mar. 2021, history.nycourts.gov/case/people-v-weeks/.

strange that they are responded to in equal ire and lack of empathy for anyone involved. Even after Constance comes home, women from the village love to call on her to tea, to look at the house and to scrutinize this acquitted murderer. There is hardly ever any kindness in this inquiry, but there is always curiosity. In this way, these famous or infamous women are also alienated from other members of their sex. Women's worlds get smaller when they are not allowed to evolve or continue, this we have seen with Kim Kardashian as her pool of people she communes with becomes smaller. Her circle also gets more dangerous as her ex-husband has shown himself to be capable of erratic behavior. The Blackwood daughter's circle gets smaller and smaller too, as outside forces take their uncle from them and part of their home. Perhaps the solution to the Kardashians and the Blackwells is similar. What would the outcome of the family be if they were to embrace radical privacy? Their money cannot refuge them from scrutiny or controversy, perhaps some silence amongst the chaos may assist them. Who can say if the town is better off now that the Blackwood girls are isolated? America and the dynamics within the Kardashian family would heal exponentially if they put away the cameras, the fear, the money, and focused inward. Where there is feminine energy, privacy to cultivate a practice, and affection, there is peace. It was Merricat's sympathetic magic practices that brought her and Constance comfort and care. It was money that brought Cousin Charles and the town to their doorstep. It was the arguing about money that brought strife to Uncle Julian and his brother. It was money that drew the Blackwell girls' mother to "The Castle."

There are eerie photos of Kris Jenner posing

protectively and cowardly behind her daughters –
guarding, protecting, and trapping – all in one photo.
What would happen to a family who feeds off our
attention and intentions if we stopped paying attention
to them and left them in the castle alone? What if they
stopped being our scapegoats for greed, sexuality, and
corruption in the United States? What if we took our
moral responsibility away from them? Would they be
nearly as powerful if they did not carry the weight of
our sins? Let us remove the mythology from them and
take back our morals. Let them live in the castle.

Michelle Belmont

Michelle Belmont is an actor and writer living in Albuquerque, NM and Los Angeles. She grew up in Olathe, KS, where she constantly annoyed her friends and family to assist her in her storytelling quests. She went on to perform in numerous plays, improv groups, and musicals in Kansas, Colorado, Australia, New Mexico and California. When she's not traveling or exploring nature with her dog, she can be found daydreaming about running away and living out a Stardew Valley-like fantasy life.

Finding My Church

I visit my homeland, a suburb outside Kansas City, in the beginning of autumn. I'm here right when despair and decay are starting to enter the air.

I describe it morbidly, but truly I love autumn, with its sweet solemnity and the contemplative air before winter descends. It's like the whole world is in pre-mourning, preparing for a winter of darkness and cold and death. It's a cyclical reminder that all must die, but also that all is reborn, that pain goes hand in hand with the act of renewing. I grew up hating the cold and winter and darkness, but I've found a new respect for it as I learn to accept the phases of life.

I'm here to visit my grandparents, as I haven't seen them since two years before. The last time I was here, I was only here briefly, to attend the funeral of the man who'd left my grandmother alone to care for their 1 and 3 year old. It's an unspoken trauma only mentioned in passing now, but one that I can see the ripple effects of to this day, even in my own interpersonal relationships.

Grandpa had reconnected with a few members of the family in the years before he died, when we could see his death was already imminent. Even before that, everyone claimed they'd all moved on and forgiven him, but I don't think he ever really felt it. I also don't really think they all felt it themselves, not really. How could they? How can you fully forgive someone who's just… not there?

Though I'm always welcome at the house of my grandparents, I know actually staying with them has gotten to be too much for them. So I take a deep breath and try to put every part of me in its proper place and stay with my childhood best friend.

In the past, this friend was practically a sister, the beginning of our lives so tightly interwound that I don't doubt we will always be in each other's lives, however distantly. But while I'm back here, in her house and in her car and in her parent's house that we visit for an evening, I find myself folding myself smaller and smaller with each passing moment, careful to not ruffle feathers or reveal just how far I've wandered off the path that they think I should be following. They ask questions, attempting to pry deeper and deeper into how I'm really living my life, what's really going on with my soul.

"Sorry, I'm going to be nosy for a little bit," leaving no room for argument. I know an argument is fruitless anyway, and instead evade the questions, putting the most talented spy dodging laser weapons to shame. I get through each sneak attack barrage of questions somehow, giving just enough information to satisfy them, but not so much that it will invite even further questioning. I'm getting better at this, at just existing, but being back here where I feel like I have to defend my every move, I just feel exhausted.

Stay small, stay good, stay quiet.

"We'll leave for church at 9:00," she says at the end of the day, not an invitation but an expectation, one that I go along with, though it feels like a betrayal.

I dutifully set an alarm, wake up, get ready, and we go. We attend the service and, though I have the formula memorized like the back of my hand (first worship, then announcements and welcome, then service, then worship again, then communion, then worship again, followed by awkward socializing), I simultaneously feel like I'm observing a social experiment gone wrong. This isn't what Jesus wanted, right? Everyone is safe and secure and fully equipped with the latest sound equipment, patting themselves on the back for their ministry, while the ones that need God's love are repeatedly ostracized and left starving outside their doors. Church was supposed to be a place of refuge, of learning, of reflection, and now they're just multimillion dollar sounding boards. I can't help but think Jesus would be flipping tables left and right if he came to the houses of worship that operate under his name.

The time for communion comes, a tradition of remembrance that's as watered down in most churches as the grape juice that's meant to represent wine, which is in turn meant to represent blood, which is absolutely as ritualistic and pagan as it sounds to anyone that didn't grow up in it.

My already shallow breath grows more strained as my friend says, not unkindly, "We didn't get you a communion cup, we weren't sure." And then suddenly I'm not sure either, and I don't even know why I have to be sure right now, in this moment. Why do I have to make a high stakes decision in the middle of unfamiliar people and an unfamiliar yet too familiar environment? I didn't ask for a crisis of faith, I'm just on this trip trying to be a good granddaughter. If I do it, if I take communion, it feels unfaithful to my sense of self, but if I don't, I know the telephone tree will light up like Christmas as the news spreads to family and friends still latched onto this vision of security they're still stuck in.

Ultimately, I choose to not partake, and preemptively brace myself for the fallout that will come weeks or years in the future.

I sit and reflect on the sermon, the flowery, welcoming words, and the sincere pleas for an arrival or return to the loving arms of God. But I also remember my friend's trepidation at anything she's not familiar with.

I remember when I got divorced and everyone's biggest fear was that I was making a mistake that would send me to Hell, not that the man that swore in front of witnesses to never hurt me was the reason I cried myself to sleep at nights for weeks on end.

I remember being thirsty for wisdom, desperate for a tender heart and compassionate words. I sought it endlessly; in the places they told me to find it. I checked the boxes, I begged for counsel, only to be brushed off, to be told that I should be running to the arms of Jesus instead. Running to the arms of Jesus was okay as a concept, but had no real-world implications, it had no meaning to a person in so much pain she couldn't determine what was real anymore.

The main problem was, in the midst of the fear and the panic and the forced blind faith, an attempt at some type of control in the face of uncertainty, I'd lost track of this "Jesus" they kept telling me to run to.

"That's between you and your husband, that's none of our business," my last- ditch attempt at connecting to wisdom told me, and I finally knew then how terribly alone I was.

In the final days, mere moments before the final divorce papers were signed, I was challenged to go off and pray about what to do, a pre-filled answer already waiting in the challenger's head. More expectations, more chances for me to disappoint.

Being a people pleaser, I sought to comply. I went to seek silence, to beg for wisdom one last time from the endless void. I would seek an answer, but I would do it my way. I went to the only place that's actually brought me peace: in the heart of nature, where being at the foot of a tree was the closest I'd ever felt to being at the feet of any god.

I sobbed and I pleaded, and I threw it all to the air, and almost immediately the air answered softly:

"Be free."

So, I set myself free, and I never looked back.

I'm not the first to find an escape route. My social media friends feed is filled with those that left the confines of the church, just like I was warned might happen to me if I wasn't faithful enough.

I see their anger, the hurt they're processing. I feel with them the injustice of a sheltered existence, I resonate with the rage that makes them retaliate against any mention of religion. I understand, and I've felt it too, but this also doesn't feel like a place to live either.

I want peace, I want love, and I want everyone around me to feel it, too. I crave the connection that was promised to me, though I want it to look different than that which is being presented as the only true option.

But being here, being back where the tendrils of this guilt-ridden existence first started to take root in my young and pliable mind, reminds me of all the times freedom was dangled in front of me in a way that was completely inaccessible to me.

In the middle of this church, my body is catapulted back in time to endless church services similar to the one I'm sitting in now. My body is back to being a teenager, disassociating during a sermon, wondering afterwards what is wrong with me that I can't pay attention enough to let the supposedly healing words penetrate my sinful mind.

All throughout my young life, I'd listen to the people gather after church, raving: "That was an amazing sermon, right?" And I'd nod my head solemnly in agreement, scrambling desperately to recall anything from what I'd spent the last 45 minutes listening to. Even just the smallest quote will get me off the hook, will color me the right shade in their eyes so that I can continue to chameleon along with their existence.

I'd observe as people swayed with inspired movement and arms lifted in reverie, wondering what was wrong with me that God chose not to touch my heart like he touched theirs. "Open your heart, let the spirit move you," I'd hear over and over.

And yet I felt nothing, always an observer, never chosen for participation.

And the guilt. That omnipresent, ever-faithful, all-seeing guilt. Why wasn't I right? Why wasn't I good? Why wasn't I who they wanted me to be?

"Do you want the pink pen?"

I'm jolted back to reality, to the present, to my friend offering me a writing utensil to fill in the sermon notes. They're passed out at the beginning of the sermon by the greeter with the distracted smile at the front of the church. These sermon notes are fill-in-the-blank style, like a worksheet a teacher hands you when they've decided to phone it in for the day and give everyone an easy A.

I politely decline the use of a writing utensil, indicating my lack of desire to fill out this worksheet, and know I've just personally handed her another nail for my coffin. But I just can't afford to expend any further energy caring.

I don't belong here, and I don't think I'm supposed to.

I go to a pond the next day, a respite in the midst of modern midwestern suburbanism, and see the fingerprints of divinity everywhere I look.

I see it in the sun twinkling through the trees, the frog poking its head out of the moss to observe me, in the smell of the earth enveloping me.

I can feel everything in me release, as my senses finally feel aligned and my soul lights up with the sparkle of finally feeling at home. I am grateful that I've returned to the wildness, where I belong, where the expanse of nature will never make me feel like I need to shrink myself to belong.

I know people lie awake at night, praying for my freedom, not knowing that I've already found it.

Please stop trying to save my soul, I'm closer to heaven than I've ever felt.

Caidyn Curry

When Caidyn is not writing in her book, "(Almost) Everything I've Ever Felt," she is playing pool or doing karaoke! She is from Albuquerque, New Mexico, born and raised. It is beautiful, but anyone who lives here knows you must get creative with your hobbies. Her current poems will be straight out of her books, which was inspired, and is now dedicated to her sister.

Dressing Room

I love shopping for clothes
Finding a new outfit
Trying them on
Until I don't like it

I found some cute pants
I got a small size
I look in the mirror
What's wrong with my thighs?

I was just wearing a six
When did this change occur
Am I too big, or just unfit?

My mom uses an excuse
"It depends on the brand
The sizes don't match
That's all honey, don't be mad."

I can't help but be frustrated
I ignore it for now
Time to get out of the dressing room
Can't keep my head down

I put the pants back
Let me check the other rack.

SAMANTHA NAGEL

I found a cute shirt
Pink and a little too tight
It will lift my boobs
When I'm out for the night

I take it to the dressing room
Try to pull it over my head
Feels comfortable at first
Too tight is the trend

It's the trend, right?

Does it shape my body
Or am I getting too big
This mirror is my enemy
Dysmorphia is setting in

Get over yourself
I tell my thoughts
My body is just different
Look at what you've got

I try to forget
I walk out of the dressing room
I put the clothes back
Next stop the bathroom

I take a good look
I have to stay strong
My mother is waiting

Holding it back, I hum my favorite song

It was the bathroom mirror
That lifts up my chin
I can only see my face
Not if I'm thick or I'm thin

A tear rolls down a groove
Created by the last
I think I hate myself
Those pants had an impact

I'm sorry to myself
For hurting my own feelings
It wasn't my intention
To fall apart because of those jeans

I've decided I'll go to bed
No dinner again
It isn't an issue
I won't do this again.

Until the next time I go into the dressing room

SAMANTHA NAGEL

Color

Black is a color, too.
In fact, black is every color
Some objects have the ability
To absorb every. Single. Color.

I promise the clouds in your mind
The soul that creates your life
The heart in your chest
Those things are not black.

They're every experience
Every. Single. Experience.
And you are colorful.

Spilled Milk

So much tension
It's built up
Give me a reason
To not cry over this cup

This spilled milk
Is not why I'm going insane
It's everything that came before
It's the rest of the pain

I was already emotional
Anything could break me
I didn't think spilling liquid
Would be the cause of my insanity

So, no, it really isn't that I spilled my milk
It's that all I wanted was to enjoy the glass
But instead, adding to other inconveniences
Every negative emotion spilling out, at last.

SAMANTHA NAGEL

Untitled

I'm not going to remember
The exact things that were said
I'm not giving you an example
Of why I felt the way I did

It's not the words you spoke
But the way they made me feel.

That's why I remember
My feelings are untitled.

Individuality

There are days
I feel most myself
When I smile
When I dance
When I do embarrassing things
To make people laugh.
But I get that from my mom…
When I remember to trust my gut
When I move like no one is watching
Pretending there is a catwalk, I strut
When I can say no
When I am self-aware
But I get that from my sisters…

When I feel anxiety
It causes me to tremble
When I take a breath
When I forget about it by being artsy
But I get that from my dad…
How will I ever know
I am doing something for me?
My beautiful insides
Made up of everybody
What are the things
That make me
Me?

Authentic

One thing that separates me
From the rest of humanity

Putting my heart on my sleeve
Yet, no one can touch me

I am loud, outgoing, and bubbly
Knowing many people, I've learned empathy

I love who I am
Even if I struggle with individuality.

Done Pleasing

People tell me to be quiet
But once I am, I'm asked if something is wrong

People tell me to stop dancing
But when I do, people tell me to move

No one wants me to be me
Except for myself
But I am one to please
So, I listen and absorb

Until I am told to speak

It feels like I try and try
To make people smile

Until I see my own face
And realize they took mine
Moving at the wrong pace
My own heart needs to be defined

My energy is fading
My heart is breaking
I've started hating
I'm only getting smarter;
my life has started shaping

Extent

No one loves to the extent
That I am capable of loving.

I am not like everyone else
They say they're not ready and start running.

My love feels so deep
Dense, causing me to drown.

In my own sorrows
I want to find what you found.

Making you my priority
My favorite hobby was making you laugh.

I thought maybe it was enough
Could claim my spot as other half.

For someone I love
I would permanently mark my skin

With beautiful pictures
Art on my arms, to represent them.

I would write a book
Every word that triggers a feeling.

Would make sure to notice

All the little changes, but for you was fulfilling.

All I want is the security
The trust, have yet to experience honest love.

Not just holding hands
Going on cute dates, but it was just lust.

I deserve what I give
The same amount, same extent.

Can't Deal

The one thing I can't stand
Is when I make someone mad
Can we just talk about it
Can I try to fix what I did
I don't want to feel this way
Any longer than I have to
What is there that I can say
To reach the happy you
I didn't even know I did anything wrong
The time I am not able explain things makes time
so long
I'm sorry if it's just me, or if that's how you truly
feel
The longer I have to wait, the harder it gets to deal

Brain vs Heart

Logic vs Emotion
Explanation vs Reaction
Thoughts vs Feelings

Every day is a struggle
I'm not unintellectual
My heart often just feels full

I know I can make logical decisions
But my heart has my next vision

Topic: Abandonment issues
Why is it so easy for them to win
And so hard for me to lose
I know I don't need them
They don't benefit my survival
But my heart created a connection
Yet, true intentions start to reveal
I need to rid them from my life
They're only making it worse
But those heart strings start to break
My heart feels it's been pierced
I can feel my heart break
Can you feel it, too?
Why did you leave me?
Was it that easy for you?

Topic: Anger
I know I should take a breath
I understand I can get over it
But screaming feels so good
Negative energy disbursing like it should
This burning inside of me
Cannot be put out with water
It must burn until the flames fade
If not, how can I ever escape?
You put water on the fire
The next thing that happens
Is smoking, a lot of smoke
The fire may be gone
But the feelings still need to be cloaked
I heard I should just take a breath, no.

Topic: Making a mistake
I know I did something wrong
I've heard I should give myself grace
But I turned down the wrong path
And hurt someone, ruined their day
That hurts me, and ruins mine
But that's how you get through life, right?
I will not forgive myself
Not until I am forgiven by you
I know mistakes are normal
But to fix things, what can I do?
I want to find a solution
I know you like your space
But I can't stand the tension

This is something I wish to erase.

Topic: Smiling
Logic and heart
Is not limited to negativity
Even when I'm happy
I react by being bubbly
Some people tell me I'm too loud
Or that I dance too much
When I was little that wasn't a thing
If you were dancing, that was a plus
I feel silenced now
Especially during the happy times
I try to be positive
But I'm being excessive
Please stop telling me my laugh
Is overbearing, understand that.

SAMANTHA NAGEL

Maybe

Maybe in another life
I would eat breakfast every day.

Maybe in another life
I could have a better career
Without needing to go to school
Without learning how to use tools.

Maybe in another life
I'm the man who broke my heart
Or the man I trusted enough
To read this art.

Maybe in another life
My parents had what I did
Now I'm growing up
I really miss them.

Maybe in another life
I would stop thinking about another life
But it seems as if new beginnings
Are not able to escape my mind

Maybe in another life
I would love mine.

03.03.2024

I cried in my car today
Listening to a song
To my parents', I was on the way.

This song, the title, the lyrics
I wish I could hear it for the first time again,
It had me tearing up, losing it

I couldn't imagine my soft life
Without who I was thinking of
As I was going on this drive

My sister, I thought about
Immediately I knew there was a real reason
To write this book, no doubt

In her hands for her to control
I would put the solar system
My world would be perfect
and I'd know where I come from.

I couldn't even try to explain
There are not enough words to say
Sister, because of you I love
Because of you I give
I always rise above
With empathy, I live.

Those words couldn't make you understand
Unconditional love, in my heart, created by your
hands.

I could say all the things
Every guy says to a girl
Cheesy things that would make one smile
Things like, you're my world

But that could never describe
The way I truly feel
You are not just my world
But because of you I pour milk before my cereal.

I see a lot of you in myself
I look in the mirror and I see your heart
But yours is much bigger than mine
It wasn't just created, but a work of art.

Imaginary Friend

I used to have one
He was my little brother
I created him in my mind
Cause I only grew up with sisters

He was a little bit younger than I was
And he stayed only in my head
But we talked all the time
He was my best friend

I had a brother until I was thirteen
Then I found some real friends
To this day I still feel bad
Not only just my friend, but on him I could
depend.

I felt safe, him in my mind
I would laugh and I would cry

He would be there to say
Anything that made bad thoughts go away.

Now he's gone forever
I've grown too much for him to stay
Adults can't have imaginary friends
I hear that means something's wrong with their
brain.

So sadly, I got rid of him
I just wish I gave him a name

Wishes

I wish I was the older sister.
I wish that growing up, I had my father.
I wish I had more money.
But not the amount that makes you snobby.

I wish I had a real talent
Not one that's usual
Like singing or dancing
But one that could be usable
I wish I was a dog or a cat
I wish I wasn't human, let's leave it at that.

I wish my government didn't ruin my future
Because now I'm lost, no child or health care.
I wish I wasn't a woman
Not one that was into men
I get all of my confidence from them
Yet, they make me feel like life should end.

Maybe I'm being a little dramatic
But I wish I wasn't so emotional
I wish I didn't wish for others
All I do is wish for lovers.
One day I will wish to be grateful.
I wish my idea of gratitude was a bit more stable.

Forgotten

That deep feeling
Spent so much time
Continuous thoughts and dreams
Them in my mind

I thought ours intertwined
Even the most minimal amount
Things block your thought from me
What were you thinking about?

I knew I wasn't the most important
But I thought I might come second

We are just friends,
I totally get that
But when did that end
To not even be that

I made it clear
That I understood
And you made it clear
What I gave you was good

It was good enough for you
Some part of me thinks you still think of me, too.

You told me you would walk me to my car.

But now I've sat here forgotten.
This experience will scar my heart.
Future negative experiences have already set in.

You told me I should expect a call back
How long will I have to lay here
As these minutes turn to hours, they stack
Waiting so long falling asleep, causing
nightmares

Now anytime I don't get a text
Anytime my favorite color isn't remembered
I don't get told Happy Birthday
I'm forgotten.

Tired from 03.04 – 03.16

I'm tired
I've been tired
I've been busy
Spinning, dizzy

I've been tired
As in it's been a while
But I haven't been tired
As in this tired

I've never been fond of sleep
I always thought it was a waste
Spending so much time in a dream
Now like water, my mind has been displaced

I'm tired
I need to sleep
Resting sounds nice
To close my eyes

I fall in love
With the idea
Of slipping
Into a short coma

Waking up
Feeling refreshed

SAMANTHA NAGEL

It's been two weeks
I want to feel it again

I'm tired
I've been tired
But I want to sleep
I want to drift

Next time I get the chance
I'm going to lie in bed
No talking, no contact
Just resting my head.

Poetry

I write poetry
I like it
I can think straight
Seeing my vulnerability

Everything spilled on the paper
But it upsets me sometimes

I write poems about love
About people
And the way it's so deep
The incisions in my heart

Incisions from everything
It has been through a lot
But I love my scars
They remind me that the past is real

I just wish one was about me
Not me writing about me
But hearing from your point of view
I want to know what you think, what you see

I want to feel like I compel you
To write these beautiful words

I want to know I'm worthy of a poem

SAMANTHA NAGEL

A written piece of art
Words written on paper
Coming straight from the heart

I am easy to open up
So, on paper it's always easier
Other people put walls up
But I just want to be eager

But somehow
One way or another
Your name commits itself to my paper
And you have compelled me to write you poems.

Age

It's not my age.

I just have questions no one can answer because I
have thoughts not even I can conceal.

It's not my age.

Music is just my passion, so if I listen to Elvis
Presley and
name my car after a Police song it's because I feel
the sounds and imagine the words.

It's not my age.

I know I'm making mistakes. But some of these
"mistakes,"
I will not learn from. Some of these (what you
call) mistakes
put smiles on other people's faces and make me
who I am.
It's not my age.

I'm not emotional because I'm a young woman.
Well, yeah
that's a reason, too. But the reason I feel broken is
because my heart has repeatedly broken in two.

It's not my age.

In fact, at my age a serious relationship isn't
something we look for. I've messed around, I've
had my time…
but I just want to be in love. Authentic love.

It's not my age.

I'm not overly empathetic because I haven't been
broken enough. I'm overly empathetic time and
time after I've been hurt. Because no one deserves
to feel like I do when I am
hurt.

It's not my age.

So stop saying that I am who I am
Because I'm twenty
I am who I am
Because experiences, I've had plenty
I may not understand your life
Your situation
Your love
Your relationship
But I understand how you feel
And I need people to stop saying I don't

It's not my age. It's just who I am.

I Miss You

To my ex-best friend. I miss you.
To my godfather in the clouds. I miss you.
My auntie who never failed to put a smile on my
mother's face when I couldn't. I miss you.
The girl from fifth grade; I was able to save her
life. I miss you. I hope you're doing okay.
To my group of coworkers that stayed late after
our shift just to be kids. I miss you.
My sister, who moved away. Only five hours, I
shouldn't complain. But I miss you.
My ex-boyfriend. Immediate chaos brought our
relationship to an end. But I miss you.
My first love. My first trustworthy companion. I
miss you.
My crush that I had in the ninth grade. We still
talk every day. I miss you.
To the friend I can't remember the name of. We
used to text when our moms had flip phones. I
miss you.
My imaginary brother I never named. I miss you.
My first best friend. We still see each other. But I
miss you.
My bunny I can hardly remember because I was
so young.
Oreo. I miss you.
My journal that only opened with a spoken
password. That was THE SHIT growing up. I

never wrote real things; I was
too young to understand the benefit of journaling.
I miss you.
My first credit card. A faint memory of the picture
on your front. I miss you.
My truck. My beautiful truck I was blessed to be
gifted. I miss you.
The Impala my mom traded for a Chevy Cruze. I
miss you.
My twelve-year-old self. With her first real
phone. When my smile in a picture didn't
dissatisfy the way I felt about my teeth. So happy.
So loving. So care-free. I miss you.
My first job. Throwing pizza dough around. I miss
you.
To the cello I used to play almost flawlessly. I
miss you.
The first songs I learned to sing. I wish I could
remember. I miss you.
It's not that I miss all these things all the time. But
a piece of me has gone missing since these things
left.
Luckily the beautiful thing about life is, as I get
older, I find replacements. Although, some things
will never compare, and some things are my new
creation for future. When I feel something
missing, I miss it temporarily. But I think about
those things often. Or I don't. But when I do, I
miss them.

People

I love people.
I love loving people.
I love relying on people,
and being relied on by people.
I love making people laugh,
and laughing.
I love telling them they're loved,
cause when they smile, I do, too.
I love thinking about people,
and being thought about.
I love it when people dance.
I love it when people race their cars on the
highway.
I love when people get married,
gosh I sure hope that for me one day.
I love getting hurt,
because without it I couldn't identify care.

I love seeing people sleeping comfortably.
I love people roller skating or skateboarding
down the street.
I love seeing all the different kinds passing the
university.
I love that people have different perspectives.
creating different personalities.
I love that a timeline of someone's past can give
you insight,
answers to the things you wonder.
I love that I can relate, but I love that I can't
understand,

my best friend taught me that.
I love selfish people.
Old people.
Aggressive people.
"Weird" people.
Emotional people.
Strong, weak, rich, and poor people.

I love people who try.
I love that people create relationships,
not only with other people,
but animals, and even objects.
I love Swedish Fish and Circus Peanuts because
I think of
My Dad.
I love the color blue and enchiladas because I
think of
My Mom.
I love honey and a well written poem because I
think of
My Hailey.
I love tequila shots (Hornitos only) and yogurt
parfait because I think of
My Jonee.
I love everything, really.
Everything has a connection to a person I was
once connected with.
I love people.
Sometimes I wish I felt this sense of love from
people.
Because I love people the way I want to be
loved.

Guilt Trip

You can't anymore.
It worked when I was younger.
Feeling stressed or guilty herself
She tried to hurt me, my mother.

As I grow older,
I can tell she's gotten older too.

It's my first time on earth
Living a life
But it's hers, too
That's why her words clouded my mind.

In some ways I am sorry
To my beautiful mother
Even though her words have changed
I didn't have much of a father.

She would disagree now,
I mean I do, too, he's great.

Growing up, she was him.
But she was guilty.

She didn't give me
Everything I could've had
But I will never forget

She always gave me what I needed.
I wish I didn't think of her negatively
But sometimes I just do
I think of the times she really hurt me
Yet I was to blame, sent to my room.
Growth is a phenomenal thing
Her and I have done it together
She did guilt trip me
But she is the one who told me not to change for
anybody.
In ways, she's to blame.
The reason I talk too loud or stand impatiently.
But she's the reason I smile bright and like
learning.
She's the reason I love. She's the reason I'm great.

She may have flaws, like playing victim. But
she's
The reason I have a life and I stay positive.
Mom, in a way, I'm guilt tripping you.

In Another Life I

I wish to be the words on these pages.
The depth of vulnerability in these poems.

In Another Life II

I want to be the music produced in a symphony.
I want to be the vibrations the orchestra creates.

In Another Life III

I hope I can be at peace.
Living whatever life I'm blessed with, serene.

SAMANTHA NAGEL

Vision Board

I've decided to create a vision board
With messages and objectives
If I complete my goals, it becomes a reward

Ripping pictures out of magazines
Something I haven't seen
The flowers glued to the page
Represent the beauty in my rage

Just pick something I want
To be able to say
Maybe this vision board
Will begin to change my ways.

Chocolate Cake

Double chocolate
Taste so deep
So rich and dense
Like the big blue sea

Chocolate cake
Mimics my brain

Mimics my heart
Mimics my pain

Still, I take these bites
Because feeling something is better than nothing.

You think double chocolate tastes good?
It does.
But that cake
So dense
So thick
Sticking to the roof of your mouth
Now I'm realizing
Maybe feeling nothing
Is better than everything.

But when I'm in need
I seek my double chocolate rich delicious cake.
Feeding myself, so my soul can become deep, just
like it.

No Rules to Love

Why am I being told enough?
Is there even rules to love?
Or am I just being judged?

My experiences are mine to experience.
Please keep it to yourself, your ignorance.

Souls

Glowing auras
Connecting universally
It's quite unbelievable
The amount of people you never meet.

But you will meet
The people you're supposed to
What's meant to cross your path
Will always come to you.

Meeting you was the most amazing thing.
In every universe, you're meant for me.

Rhyme

This poem is about rhymes.
It isn't too hard
I do it all the time.

Don't get me wrong,
It can get difficult sometimes.

To try and find
These hidden words
In my mind.

I go through the pages
Line for line

Which words actually align?

They don't even have to be perfect:

Lemons and limes.
Quarters and dimes.

My brain is trying to unwind.
These strings, intertwined.

I've whined and I've cried.
All my vocabulary collides.

Until my pen glides.

On paper I write.

I'm becoming blind.
To my own pride.

My ego is high.
Poetry is my guide.

It's begun to take over my life.
Stuck in a loop of time.

I need to take a step outside.
But I'm in a bind.

Because it isn't too hard
I do it all the time.

Gen Z

Known as lazy
When I was told
At a very young age
I'd be free
Now dumbfounded
But not for long
We can all see
The way we were betrayed
By our own family tree
We aren't lazy
We are waiting
For the promises

The guarantees
To finally be
Followed through
We are not lazy
But what is the reason for living
If I am working
Not two, but three
Jobs are hard enough
When you're barely getting by
But barely getting by
And not having any me time
We are not lazy
But too willing to give our all, yet the minimum
is what we
receive.

Glue is a Girl's Best Friend

Glue is a girl's best friend
Diamonds are just a trend
Don't get me wrong, they're pretty
But glue is a necessity.

Diamonds may be strong,
But it's glue I use to keep my eyelashes long.

I use glue for my nails
For small tears in my wedding veil.

Glue on my fingertips
Stuck to the perfect position on my hips.
Stuck, just like glue
Since the moment I met you.

Usually, what I look like is what it benefits
But now it's on my lips.

And every time I kiss you
It keeps me from backing away, the glue.

Glue is a girl's best friend
Until you're the one that buys the diamond.

Glue is what keeps me put together.
Because of it, I have you forever

Idea

I love the idea of you.
But you are not what I had in mind.

The things that you do.
But others unravel with time.

I love the version
I created in my head.

It isn't your fault
But you changed since the first time we met.
I thought I loved you. But it was the idea of being
loved
instead.

Fatigued

I'm not saying no one else is
But I've become selfish
I think of my busy days
All of them feel the same

I'm getting tired and restless
Been trying to fix this
Motivation dissolves every second
My to do list is constant

I walk into my bedroom every day
I just see the bed where I lay
But not the dirty dishes
Or the laundry that has perished

I need to take the trash
Go to the gym and take a bath
I feel ashamed for being lazy
But I have another priority

It is killing me inside
Making excuses to hide
Something I need to get finished
But I hear "it's okay to be selfish"

I was told a couple days ago
I'm tired, not the way you think you know

And all I could do was support and act intrigued
When I know that exact feeling, fatigued

Rest and sleep always sound nice
But a break from stress is what I emphasize
I'm not tired from working
But tired that is the only way to survive

I'm tired of loving so hard
I'm tired of people telling me I don't understand
When I feel what they do when I touch their hand
I touch their heart
With my heart
Now broken in two and two again
For trusting people, no hesitation
There is no restraint on the feelings I have
I want to give more love than I get back
I've fatigued myself trying to please
When I get home, I fall to my knees
I pray to the God I've never known
The God I don't know if to believe
Hoping I'm given guidance to grow.

Sara Saint-Hogan

Sara was born and raised in Northern New Mexico. She's the author of The Enchanted Ones, Book 1: The Greater Good - the first of a trilogy. She has also published other things under a pen name. She's currently a teacher at a small rural school in Northern New Mexico, teaching primarily students with dyslexia how to read. She is married and has one son and four cats.

This is a story about how a girl who was once strongly connected to nature became disconnected from it through fear indoctrination and undiagnosed ADHD. It's also about how she, now a woman, is learning to reconnect to the parts of herself that were once so sacred. This is a story of how she looked for belonging in all the wrong places, only to realize that she belongs to her own true self.

As a child, I cherished the magic of nature. My grandmother took me for walks around our small town and into the surrounding woods. We cawed at the crows and played "poor," which entailed gathering leaves, sticks, flowers, and rocks to bring home. As I got older, my cousins or friends went with me, and we explored, made forts, and other things that kids normally do in the woods. But, when I went on my own, I often lost myself in the wonder of it. I lost all sense of time and responsibility. I was often found staring at the sky, animals, or flowers. I spent hours watching the moth larvae making their way back up trees on a single silk thread. I got lost watching the ants carrying things far larger than they were back to their ant holes.

I often walked or rode my bike the half mile to school. One day, I arrived late. When the teacher asked where I had been, I simply replied, "There was a frog in the road," as if that was a perfectly valid excuse that needed no further justification. My return trips home were usually delayed by something fascinating in nature that completely enthralled my attention, like the spinning of water down the hole in the manhole cover after a rainstorm. That was just who I was. But it didn't make my teachers, parents, aunts, or uncles very happy, though.

I vividly remember being asked once to stand outside our building to direct people to the theater, where we were having a piano recital. I wasn't told how long to wait or how many people were coming. It was just starting to snow, and I got completely lost in staring upward and feeling the light flakes on my face. I remember catching them on my tongue and fingers and watching them melt. I was completely fascinated by the magic of the season's first snow. But then I was suddenly ripped out of my revelry by my mom grabbing my arm and shouting that I made the recital start late because I was busy daydreaming. And my piano teacher was also unhappy with me when I returned to the theater. I wanted to explain that they didn't tell me how many people were coming, and it was snowing! But I knew there was no point. They would simply tell me I was careless, lazy, or weird.

Although daydreaming was a gift of mine, I also had undiagnosed ADHD. So, my ability to get completely lost in nature was exaggerated. I daydreamed through entire lessons at school. But when I was outside in the woods surrounding our town, I was in a completely different world. And when I was with someone my age, I got them to completely immerse themselves in the magic and mystery of it as well. I used to believe that I had a connection with the forest fairies, elves, and other forest entities. Also, I believed I had possessed magical powers in a past life that only nature could give. I simply hadn't remembered how to use them. Later, I feared this was because I was being punished for misusing them in a past life.

When you have attention issues, remembering to do simple things is quite a task. Learning how to stimulate healthy dopamine responses in your brain as a psychological reward becomes even more important. Not realizing this, I started seeking dopamine rewards from artificial sources, like video games, computers, and later social media. This slowly severed my connection to nature. Worse still, I was regularly cautioned by my aunt and uncle to avoid nature beings like fairies and elves. I was told they inhabited "bad" realms and that if I saw them, I would "get into serious trouble" and need to be "cleaned up energetically." And having convinced the entire family that they were enlightened gurus, I felt obliged to listen to them. At the same time, they proudly encouraged their children, *my cousins*, to see fairies and elves.

Then, life happened. I went to college and got married. I completely forgot about the hours I spent staring at the trees, sky, little bugs, and other critters. I forgot that I used to feel nature talking to me. I forgot that I am part of nature, and got caught up in other things. The impression that I was somehow "weird" became part of my identity. But I wasn't really weird; I was just a child with her head in the clouds. Despite that, I gradually became "grounded" and "successful," staying away from things "dangerous." My grandmother later confessed to me that she was genuinely concerned about me because I was "so out there." And she was extremely proud of how successful I became despite my oddness.

I raised a child and realized how disappointed I was that I hadn't instilled a love for nature that I once cherished. I tried to get him to spend time outdoors as a child. But he was a high-needs child who didn't speak coherently until he was four. And I worked full-time as a teacher. So, during the week, he was either with his dad, who was raised in the big city and didn't spend much time outside (at the time), or his grandma (my mom), who was afraid to leave the house. Ultimately, I have myself to blame, though, because I allowed myself to get "indoctrinated" by a modern, disconnected, "rational" society. But I must've done something right because he's an easy-going teen who is well-liked by just about everyone who's met him.

He's actually a lot like me in that regard. I was the good kid, the "goody two shoes." I went with the flow and was highly impressionable. Yet, I had a high sense of morality. For instance, knowing that drugs would ruin my still-developing brain, I refused them. As a result, I was ridiculed by some of my friends. I was told to "be a rebel," "live a little," and "it wouldn't hurt me that bad." I didn't even drink any alcohol until

I was nearly eighteen. Even then, I didn't get drunk until I was twenty-one. I tried pot in college, but I liked it way too much to keep doing it, so I stopped. To this day, I rarely drink, maybe once or twice a year. Unfortunately, this isolates me from my community. To make friends here, you either have to attend one of the churches or hang out at the bar. I've never had any interest in either, though.

Being an introvert, I don't need to get drunk or high to have fun. And though I believe in God, I have no use for organized religion. When my friends tried to get me to go to church, I felt incredibly uncomfortable. I was used to "fear indoctrination" from my childhood. But the kind of fear the churches instilled in their members made me feel sick to my stomach.

In college, my friends and roommates tried to get me to attend church. One even said, "You need a church, any church. How else will you communicate with God? You can't do it on your own." To placate her, I agreed to go with her to several different non-denominational churches to help me find one that "fit me." She disliked all of them. And the one that appealed to me the most, Unitarian Universalists, she especially disliked because they didn't mention Jesus once during the entire sermon. In the end, she realized that I probably wouldn't attend church anyway and gave up.

I absolutely loved college but initially had trouble fitting in there as well. I eventually found a like-minded friend my freshman year, and we were inseparable until she moved away after she graduated. During our time together, we kept our feet on the ground and our heads in the clouds.

She was there for me when I was dating someone with a dark side. He eventually admitted to practicing black magic and introduced me to his mentor, who promptly told him he had messed with the wrong person. He explained that there was a strong protection around me, and my protectors would not be kind to him if he harmed me. He told him I was unique in ways he would never know or appreciate and to leave me alone. I always assumed these protectors were my aunt and uncle. But in retrospect, I'm not so sure it was them. Now, I wonder if it was my latent connection to nature that somehow protected me.

Growing up, I was taught that any teachings outside of what my gurus taught were either incomplete or incorrect. Only they and a handful of others could give the proper initiation that would lead to enlightenment. Everyone else was "lost in maya." My gurus believed they had been given the "correct" teachings by someone who claimed to be Jesus and the Buddha in past lives. Other teachings were "unsafe" and couldn't be studied concurrently with theirs.

Unfortunately, this type of "fear indoctrination" is hereditary in my family. My mother's maternal grandmother had agoraphobia and suffered debilitating migraines when she got home after shopping at the local market. My mother's paternal aunts were afraid of everything and tried to project that fear onto their kids, nieces, and nephews. "Get in the house; you're afraid of dogs," was a quote that my mom, aunt, and uncle often made fun of. It was said by one of their aunts, who raised her children to be afraid of the world. But, in reality, I wasn't raised all that much differently.

I love my mother dearly, but she constantly worries about everything, especially the things that are beyond her control. She was overprotective and controlling when I was growing up. She doesn't realize how much she projects her fear onto others. And being a very impressionable, shy, and introverted child, I absorbed much of it. My late aunt was a saving grace in this regard. As my guru, she forced me to do the mundane things that I was taught to fear. But ironically, she instilled a great fear in me of exploring the spiritual path in my own unique way.

So, where do I go from here? I'm not entirely sure yet. I've made a beginning by acknowledging my fear of discovering my destiny. I'm also revisiting free-verse poetry I wrote when I was younger, especially those focused on nature or spirituality. I've also started taking a lot of nature pictures and spending more time just sitting in nature and listening to what it has to say. I'm reaffirming the parts of myself I suppressed in order to fit in. I'm no longer caring what others think of me. I know there's a valid reason that I'm different. And I must look within to discover why.

I'm including some of my free-verse poetry. Most of my poems were written when I was a teen through my early twenties, so they are pretty rudimentary and unedited, but I think they show how connected I was to those parts of myself I tried to suppress. No one outside my close friends or family has read these, so I feel a little vulnerable about sharing them.

Mysteries (fall 1994)

The wind blows silently through the trees.
Darkness falls like a thick blanket.
The night has the sense of mystery and danger.
A lone wolf calls out to the full moon.
My heart begins to bound as I near the river's edge.
The water seems unnaturally still in the darkness
I can see the wolf standing on a ledge,
silhouetted by the luminous moon.
I call out to him and he stops his call to the moon.
He looks my way, then disappears in the darkness.
I begin to walk stealthily beside the river's edge.
I hear a splash into the river's water,
and soon the wolf joins me.
I can hear his heavy breathing and my own heartbeat
begins to quicken in anticipation of the
night's mysteries.

SAMANTHA NAGEL

Silence (unedited 9/13/1997)

Silence…
Warm breezes fill the air
Sweet scents float along
Silence…
Leaves rustle with the breeze
Silence…
The dark sky lights up with lightning
Silence…
A sense of comfort,
Easiness, relaxation,
Tranquility, beauty
Silence

Silence (edited 9/13/1997)

Warm breezes fill the air
Leaves sing melodically for all to hear
Sweet scents of rain float,
Adrift on invisible streams
Distant city lights paint the softly clouded midnight
sky
A sense of peace, tranquility, beauty
(A calming comfort, beauty in tranquility)
Silence

SAMANTHA NAGEL

It is Time (8/8/1999)

Light fills the room of my soul
It fills me with inexplicable joy
This is the healing light
It heals my past hurts and wounds
I know I can help others with this light
It brings all of us home
Tears of joy flood my eyes
The New Age is here
He calls us to HIM – call us home
Colors of the softest kindness float above
I am lifted up into Love
Paradise has reached us
It is time of us to the answer the call
It is Time

Untitled (3/5/2001)

Sound exceeds Time
Life brings forth new Meaning
The Earth
The Universe
Physical bodies watch the Dawn
The Dawn of Change
Sound exceeds Time
Without a trace, it is gone
It is here
Time brings Death
Death of Old
Birth of New
Watch
Wait
Listen
Sound brings Peace
Peace Inside
Harmony
Life – Light
Beauty
Beauty to see – Beauty to hear
Listen
Sound exceeds Time
Light exceeds All

Bloom 3/19/01

I am like a Rose that has not bloomed
Hiding behind childlike innocence
Too timid to show her petals
Afraid of what she could be
Comfortable within the guise of youthful beauty
Not realizing the Beauty in spiritual maturity
Having so much to offer to herself and to others
But keeping it locked behind tight petals
Afraid of losing purity,
but not realizing that true Beauty is pure
Let the petals unfold
Let the light within be known
Be true to yourself and let it shine
like a perpetual bloom
Let go, Release, and Bloom

Shyanne Martinez

Shyanne Martinez is an established fiction and poetry author, leaning more towards the romantic version of literacy. Her novels explore themes of becoming, love, and friendship. Her poetry takes a more day-to-day stance of feeling left out, navigating your 20s, and accepting who you are supposed to be. Shyanne has been writing novels since she was a child, publishing her first book at 19 years old. Shyanne proudly works with various companies providing social media management, alongside being an educator, a beta reader, advocate, and an active member of her local church. Shyanne is probably best found at a Taylor Swift concert or reading a book at her favorite local coffee shop.

Dedicated to my younger self, I'd like to think she'd find solace in who we are today. And to everyone who wonders if I'm writing about them, I probably am.

Enjoy. xx

Who I'd Be If You Kept Me Around

I think purple is a color you could use to describe me. Not because of lavender or the peace, but because I'm beaten by the conformity that is my rage. I have been angry probably every single day of my life. Is that why you find me hard to love? But I conform and I cave and I never let you see my animosity.

And that color looks different on everyone. Mine isn't dark like a hole in the wall or a red voice raised, mine is a silent, slow type of gray. The kind that pays. It tolls and it takes and the only one who's left to pay is me. With my sanity.

I don't get to keep and I don't get to fight. I have to sit with my might and bite and pray. I want to wish all of my horrors away. Everything I've ever loved has left me in some way.

I see the way I can be of use. I can spring to action, wrap a wound, heal a heart, could probably turn it back from blue. I can be whatever it is you want me to be. I can mend or stitch or recreate a lost playlist.

I think in some ways you see me too. Maybe someday I can join you. Because I blend in with the parts of my soul that are blue, but not because I like the color but because I like it on you. I wish I could fight and show my teeth snarling at my world. But instead, I smile, because I'm a good girl.

I cannot conform, and I cannot fight. I can sing, I can shout but oh— *be quiet.* I cannot stand and I cannot sit, I can simply be the person you want in the middle of it. I am not your daughter, I am not your friend. I am simply a person you've chosen to mend.

I am what you've wanted, and that's how I'll stay. I'll be this way if you need me, just promise you'll stay. I can't handle rejection, I can't handle where I'm going. I can only fear what is ahead of me because I can't control it.

Am I a person? Am I just a girl? Am I a conformity to your modern world? Am I lovable— was I ever going to be?

I think I'm perfect because I'm sculpted in the way you wanted me to be. But how can I be human if you just molded me?

I'm the Book You Return Early

My mind is a dusty library
I've seen my life run wild before my eyes
Without a single sign of stopping
I have a life that's never let me be disengaged
In a constant fight, never a chance to be still
There haven't been many moments where
The wild hasn't ripped me to pieces
Leaving the remnants of my identity in the wake
My edges are shredded
Marked with the blood from cuts I got trying to
turn pages
There are shelves I don't let myself climb
anymore
Genres that we don't talk about
No one visits libraries anymore
Would you like a free pass?

Poems I'll Never Share

the one where i admit he shoved me around or
when he
slipped a finger into the hole in my jeans
or when i stopped eating
or when he moved
and when he left
and when i left
and now anytime i feel grief
the one when i dated boys i shouldn't have
or when i tucked a ring box into my closet
or about how many people noticed i lost weight
the one when i acknowledge disordered eating
and racism
and loneliness
the one where i admitted to loving you before i
said it aloud
or to anyone in my life
or when i was a secret
one i was okay being
the one with texts i never sent
or words i never said
or things i wish i could take back
the one when i realized what he did has a name
the one where you hated your parents
or were neglected by all adults really
the one where i'd sneak off in the middle of the
night
in truck beds of someone i thought understood me
and maybe he did

the ones of lost friends
i've lost count
of the friends and the poems
the ones where i felt so alone
or spiraled into thinking i was alone
or consumed myself with isolation and avoidance
the ones where i begged
the ones where i pleaded
the ones where i was delusional
or in denial
or hopeful
the ones that will cease to exist anywhere but in
my mind
you can't have those
because then you'll have me
in your hands
and no one knows how to hold a book properly.

SAMANTHA NAGEL

Glass Bottle on a Beach

I don't really think I'm going to belong anywhere
Like maple syrup that's sitting in your fridge or
honey in
your coffee
I've chased fragments of my identity on the words
of strangers
And every time I find a corner shelf to tuck myself
into,
suddenly I'm reshelved, having to adjust to genres
that I no longer fit in with
Then I watch my history burn on your pages
So you look at me with your face of disapproval
Because I don't belong
And you would've done my life differently
So I read your poetry
And paint myself in colors you laid out
Trying to fit in—never to stand out
Stripped of anything to make me feel like I am
apart
But one thing you can't take from me is the home
I've made
from my art

Glass Bottle on a Beach (Reconfigured)

I don't really think I'm going to belong anywhere
Like maple syrup that's sitting in your fridge or
honey in
your coffee
I've chased fragments of my identity on the words
of strangers
Just let me in—I'll be your proxy
I watch my history burn on your pages
And your face of disapproval
Because you would've done my life differently
All working towards my removal
So I read your poetry
And paint myself in colors you laid out
Trying to fit in—never to stand out
Stripped of anything to make me feel like I am
apart
But one thing you can't take from me is the home
I've made
from my art

SAMANTHA NAGEL

Ways You Have Saved My Contact Info
after Michelle Awad

Girl living in a city she meant to leave over four years ago, who climbs the occasional grocery store shelf for dairy-free ice cream, *that's how you met her*. Nearing a quarter-life crisis; back-left row of a church pew, carrying a coffee and a reusable water bottle covered in Taylor Swift stickers; brown eyes that melt you like chocolate in the summer; girl who bought a copy of her favorite book for you to have, *you never read it*. Girl who cheers for your soccer team, even though she's more of a football fan; girl who asks you to make her an espresso with cinnamon, who dances in the kitchen while you bake; girl who you swear God made for you, *but you won't marry her*. Girl who touches her necklace when she's anxious, who will ask for reassurance that you enjoy her company, *you promise you do*.

You change my name in your phone to something that has
always been true:

Girl who will always have a piece of my heart

Or maybe you'll change it to something only we understand:

Something having to do with December.

Dating Profile

Located in a city she meant to leave almost four
years ago.
Standing at a height that requires her to
occasionally climb
onto a grocery store shelf
Legally allowed to rent a car, entering her quarter-
life crisis
Finds her comfort in the God of the Universe,
which means
she loves without bounds
A stunning smile that only took two years' worth
of braces
Brown eyes that have once been described as
honey meeting oak
Curly hair that's spent four years in recovery from
being flat ironed constantly from age seven
A noticeable scar on the chin that's an ode to two
left feet
Books in hand, referencing not one but two active
library cards
A-line dress, giving just enough to the
imagination to keep you interested
A reference to Taylor Swift, to weed out the anti-
feminists
Front-row at a concert, despite actually being
introverted
A joke, to make you crack a smile
Are you not entertained?

The Game of Life

I was supposed to have a wedding dress in the
closet
and a ring on my finger
and a dog in the yard
and friends on my speed dial.
Instead I have concert t-shirts
and necklaces I never take off
and a yoga mat
and a therapist.
Instead
I'm in a reality I never dreamed of.
But I'm safe
and that's got to count for something
because it's all I really wished for.

A Love Letter to My Friends

I love the friends that make you feel like you
belong
Grab my hand in a crowd
Got you an iced matcha
I'll wing your eyeliner type of girls
The ones who tell you which outfit looks good
when all you've done is change the necklace
The ones who listen to your 10-minute voice
memos in traffic
The ones who agree to split an appetizer
The cut your hair in my living room
Driving to hike at sunrise
"and another thing"
Type of girls
The fight a strange man in a bar
Grade papers while we talk
Breastfeeding in public
Type of friends
The friends whose messages you screenshot to
remind yourself how loved you are
The friends who come over with a breakup basket
and ice cream
The friends who drive across town every Monday
during rush hour so you don't have to go the gym
alone
The women who take you under their wing and
share their stories from when they were your age

The women who let you call them big sisters
because they're always the first to offer wisdom
The women who dance with you at weddings
The women who see you
Hear you
Hug you
Miss you
Sit on the bathroom counter with you
Grab your hand and say, "I'm in this with you"

Those are the women I want to embody
Those are the women who make me feel like I
belong

Even Jesus Disappointed People

An ongoing list of Bible characters facing their
humanity:
The ones like Martha, so focused on the details
than to slow down to be with Jesus
The ones like Mary, weeping at Jesus' feet, asking
him why he hadn't been there when she called
The ones like Elijah, who are tempted to give up
when all they need is a snack and a nap
The ones like Abigail, taking matters into their
own hands instead of relying on someone else
The ones like Noah, who do things that don't
make sense to everyone else
The ones like Peter, sometimes letting their anger
react first
The ones like Jesus, who begged God to change
the circumstance
Those are the ones that make me feel a little less
alone

The Culmination of Emerald Rowse

Chapter 25
For once, not doing what's expected
Chapter 24
Falling in love with someone who moved away
Chapter 23
Quitting the job she got a degree for
Chapter 22
Moved out on her own + kissing her first stranger
in a crowded room
Chapter 21
Graduating college without her best friend
Chapter 20
Error: 404 file not found
Chapter 19
Publishing her first novel
Chapter 18
Saying yes to a future she didn't want
Chapters 12-17
Archives not found
Chapter 11
Writing her first novel, based on a dream
Chapters 1-10
Archives have been lost

Alex Mirabal

Alexandra Mirabal is a woman of many interests. Born and raised in Albuquerque, New Mexico, her current list of activities includes ballroom dancing, singing in a queer doowop punk band, performing burlesque and working on her Bachelor's degree. She is happiest when she is outdoors with her partner and dogs!

Pressure

There is no greater spiritual experience than truly
being out in nature.
Standing at the base of the mountains, staring up at
the stars in the night sky, dipping your toes in the
frigid waters of the river.
In these moments, there is no need for sinners and
saints,
No angels and demons,
No pews, pulpits or holy books,
But a genuine peace.
The realization that the same elements that make up
this beauty around you, exist within you.
You stare in amazement at the beauty around you.
You think, if this beauty was created by immense
pressure and stress, what can pressure and stress do
for me.
Peace surrounds you as you feel the connection to
everything around you.
You can choose to either feel sad about how small
your role is in this great universe, or you can be
grateful to be a part of such a beautiful world

Samantha Nagel

Samantha Nagel (she/her) is a bestselling author of Nasty Woman, a poetry collection that explores hope, grief, love, loss, and, above all, the experience of learning to love oneself despite not knowing how. She loves to write fiction as well, and is working on her first novel, a sapphic contemporary romance.

Samantha is also a staff writer at New Mexico Entertainment Magazine and Pride & Equality Magazine, a community organizer, developmental editor, beta reader, and a proud member of the shadow cast of Rocky Horror Picture Show at the Guild Cinema.

Samantha lives in New Mexico with her husband and two dogs and is probably drinking too much coffee while watching Ru Paul's Drag Race or reading a contemporary romance novel and listening to Chappell Roan.

Content Guidance: The following poems contain themes of childhood sexual and emotional abuse, as well as sexual assault. Please read carefully.

My teeth are razor sharp,
My bite even worse than my bark,
Foam forming at the mouth,
But yet I never open my lips

- **tamed**

I wish I could go back to the days that we were
blind to time,
Rising with the sun,
Sleeping with the stars,
Not afraid of the dark.

- **eternal**

She would yell, she would scream,
And then when I was nothing but an empty shell,
She would gorge me full of loving bombs,
replacing the pit
in my stomach with acid guilt and putrid shame.

**My first drug was my mother's cold hatred, and
then the euphoria of her love.**

From wind in my hair to the feeling of the air
knocked out
of my chest,
I was free and then I was trapped.
From wide toothed smiles to salt soaked gums,
I was alive, and then I was numb.
From an innocent child to a ghost of an outline,
I was understood and then I was forgotten.
From dirt in my toes to blood down my legs,
I was wild and then I was nothing.

What Do I Do?

What do you do when the one who breaks your
heart first is the one whose heart beat gave you
life for 9 months,
The one whose body nourished yours as your tiny
limbs grew, inch by tender inch?

What do you do when they read parenting books,
But also stole your diaries
And used every word they read as daggers they
could use to stab you with?

What do you do when your first traumas with
capital Ts happened with the same person who
saw your first steps?
The first person who commented on my budding
breasts and supple hips was my mother,

Something I find alarming as I realize
That if a father said what my mother did,
His daughter would never speak to him again.

She didn't just notice my body,
My body was her body,
And she needed it to be perfect,

And needed to remind me of it too.

I saw a photo of myself from when I was fourteen,
A photo where I thought I was fat and picked at
my skin in the mirror, willing it to be smaller.

I looked like a skeleton with eyes that were
hungry.

Mother Gothel's Parentified Daughter

Once Upon A Time,

Lost in my own tower,
Locks on the doors,
Barbed wire hitting my lungs,
All I longed for was to know the sky

Midnight hair that reeked of bleach
t
      a
n
    g
          l
            e
            d
and
l
o
n
g,
Teeth whitening strips
And a bedroom door
That c r e a k e d open at night.

A prisoner,
Told to be grateful
"You two are so close!"

My tragedy untold.
Haunted by memories
I was told
Never Happened.

In the end,
The prince was me,
But also not me,
But it certainly wasn't
her.
I'm rewriting my happy ending.

You Don't Have to be Loved

By those who do not
Occupy a space in your heart.
You do not need to be accepted,
In order to accept the truest parts of yourself.
You are free
To love yourself,
Your true self,
Not just the mask
You hang for the audience.
You have existed in a circus,
With smokes and mirrors,
Always hiding your true self,
Always reflecting what you think
The crowd wants to see.
It is time to hold your own mirror,
To face your own reflection.
What I hope to see someday
Is a woman
Who loves herself,
Every opinion,
Every scar,
Every crooked tooth
And swollen blemish.
I hope to see a woman,
A woman who is loved.
A woman who is loved,
Not by the praise

She seeks from her critics,
Not by from the cheers
She wants from her spectators.
I hope to see a woman
Who is loved
From her chapped lipped smile,
To her dainty hands,
From her tiny toes,
To her thick thighs,
From her gentle voice,
To her savage tears.
I hope to see a woman,
Authentic,
At peace,
Loved.

Ten

yesterday I sent my newly deceased mother
10 messages that she'll never read
10 messages I would never want her to read
10 messages that all I want is for her to read
10 messages that I desperately wish she could
respond to
10 messages I'm grateful I'll never hear her
response to

October 19

An Ode to Rocky Horror

Ten years ago today
I was raped
And in the nine years since,
October makes me
Sweat
Shudder
Cringe
Cry
Hide
Hate
And other things I don't know how to say,
Despite everything I've tried

This year,
I put on my fishnet thigh highs,
My red feather boa,
Enough hairspray to become a fire hazard,
And I did the Time Warp with
My closest friends,
My new family
(And an unnerving amount of strangers)

And this year,
On the tenth year,
October didn't make me
Sweat
Shudder

Cringe
Cry
Hide
Or hate,
For the first October
In a very long time

The Loneliness of Grief

And who is there after the initial shock wave

Who will ask how you are every day for more
days than the
first few
Who offers to help once the service is over
And the ashes are mailed away
And all you're left with is fifteen copies of a death
certificate with the wrong birthdate and a hollow
feeling in your chest that most people can't
understand because most people aren't supposed
to lose their parents in their 20s,
their car parked in your driveway, their old
photographs in your basement,
The purse that you've seen them grab over and
over again on their way out the door, shoved on a
shelf
Because you can't bear to get rid of it,
 But you sure as hell don't want to look at
Who is there when it's been three weeks instead
of three days, And who is there when it's been
three months

The only one you can truly count on
Is you

Wild & Free

If I could go back to visit her
I would go back to the day when
Her laughter was filled with joy
Instead of masked discomfort.
I would long to visit the days of being her true
self,
Playing pretend alone in the arroyos,
Visiting fairy world and mountains and quests and
adventures.
I would revisit the slowness of her laying on her
back in the hills behind her house,
Blanket spread over rocks
And goat heads,
Cows grazing just beyond the crest,
Gazing at clouds above, watching them morph
and change
as we assigned them characters.

I would revisit the times she spent next to the
creek by her house,
Pant legs wet from crossing blue-green water,
Ankles sore from slipping on algae covered rocks
that lived on the bottom.
She spent those days resting on leaf beds of her
creation,
Following barely there new trails,
Watching birds and slowly and meticulously
picking up rocks for the collection,
Pretending they were gems,

And she was a queen.

The best part of her day
Was watching the butterflies dance,
Bright sun on her shoulders, feeling the freckles
of a new tan kiss her collarbones,
Spending hours on the phone with her best friend.
The most stressful part of her day
Was choosing what book to flip through first,
Which fork in the trail to follow first.

I would return to those days because they were
easy.
Only animals that were friends too,
Story book characters,
Only blisters on heels
From walking barefoot
On the hot dirt and dusty fields.

There were no parents arguing,
No pressures at work,
No rigid rules,
No male gaze,
No beauty standards,
No masks to put on,

There was just me,
Wild and free.

XIII

The night that I found out that my grandmother died, I cried,
but not because I was sad that she had passed.
I cried because my mother's mother, just like my father's
mother,
was yet another woman who died having lived an unlived
life.
I cried because I came from a line of women
that lived life being terrified of living. I cried because
most of the women I knew
came from a line of women like this.

I cried because of all the ways that my mother told me
that she never wanted to be like her mother, and I cried
because of all the ways my father told me he wished I
could have met his mother.

My tears are mine, salty, bitter, raw, but my tears are
also hers, and hers before her, and hers before her. I
cry, and I think of the tears of Demeter,
sprawled across the barren earth, mourning the loss of
her daughter, only this time, I wonder if Demeter ever
cried for her mother, and her mother's mother.
Persephone chose to eat the pomegranate seeds,

to claim her crown and sit on the throne of the Underworld, but something tells me that Demeter's grandmother, and her grandmother's grandmother, never made those kinds of bold, wild, delusional decisions.

Did you know that when a woman carries a baby girl inside her womb, she not only holds her daughter in her body, but her granddaughter, too?

Perhaps I cry because the woman where I was just a twinkling possibility in her belly has just breathed her last breath, and perhaps I cry because I am not confident that she had many breathtaking moments in her life, that she didn't have memories of laughing just to feel herself smile, or loving without thinking of the way her heart could break.

I cry to think of my father's mother, who stayed with a husband who couldn't have loved her less, just to be a good mother. She left my grandfather when my father turned eighteen, only to die a few short years later.

I own her tarot cards, the frayed edges of the Rider Tarot cards soft against my fingers, thinking of how her hands must have held what mine so gently touch.

We often cry for the person who has died, asking our version of a god why they have taken our loved one from us.

It seems it is always too soon, too painful, too quick, not quick enough.

We say *why God, why would you do this to me?* As if death is something to run from, as if it's a punishment that only our father in the sky would strike us down with.

I don't think God has anything to do with death,
If anything, Death *is* God, and God is a woman.

Mother Death is not the one to fear,
No, it is far more horrifying to consider Life as the main antagonist in this fable. For it is Life that can truly terrify us the most,
Think of the women in my family, think of the women in yours. Think of the way they tell themselves that they are not enough, not worthy of hard things, scary things, beautiful things, which by the way, are one and the same.

Is Death a skeleton wearing armor on a white horse leaving the ruble of discarded life behind it, a man on his knees in front of it, begging to live life? It is not Death that one needs to beg to live their life, it is their own tamed spirit inside the birdcage of their ribs that one must plead with.
It is the chains that our world has cuffed around our wrists,
devastating, yes, daunting, yes, horrifying, of course, but our responsibility, also yes,

that we must bargain with. For as much as I resent the truth that we must all find the feeble bloom of a morning glory that is resiliency,
it is the journey that Mother Death asks us to embark on.

No, we needn't be afraid of Death, just as a fawn need not fear the nurturing love of its mother as it waits for its offspring to learn to walk, for that too is how Death waits for us in the wings, not threatening us with Her inevitability, but reminding us of our one precious and precarious life that we deserve to live.

Oftentimes, She comes to us during our lives, to shock us,
to push us, to hold and carry us
into the next chapter, often when we have been resisting Her with our heels dug into the stone thick dirt. She comes to us like Persephone with her wrought iron crown,
    offering us those six seeds, but really,
    offering us the opportunity to not run from Death, but to run towards her, to let her hold your hand in your one waltz with Life.

Many times, when we pull the Death card, we feel frightened, looking out our windows, straining for the call of the screaming Banshee in the middle of the night, holding fast to our loved ones, wanting them to be still and to be next to us, lest we lose them.

In this desperation to hold on, we don't keep their fragile bird hearts safe,
We just keep them, doomed to living a life they won't remember on their deathbed.
When I flip through my father's mother's tarot guide book, I stare at the page marked XIII, an unlucky number for some, and a holy number for others, to see it has been dogeared, perhaps by my grandmother, perhaps by my father after his mother's passing.
"But Death is the twin brother of Life. Creation necessitates its opposite - destruction. As Spirit descends into matter, so it must return to its source. Spirit is immortal; thus humanity can never die, for the Destroyer has become the Creator."

And you, dear reader,
How will you become the Creator, your own Divine Architect
of your one life that your mother has given you?
Will you throw your body on dirt and wail against the impermanence of every beautiful thing, or will you travel into your own underworld, to hold hands with the very devastating and wonderful fact that everything you love will most definitely perish?
Will you mourn your ancestral wounds that whisper and hiss at you that you aren't worth Living, that Life will crush you, that you are far safer to shrink and hide, always moving into the shadows so that the sun won't find out,

Only to soothe them, comfort them, and ultimately
ignore them,

As you live a life your great-great-grandmother
would have only dreamt of living?

Wild & Untamed Thing

Content Guidance: The following essay contains themes of childhood sexual and emotional abuse, as well as sexual assault. Please read carefully.

"Sex, drugs, rock'n'roll, Rocky Horror Picture Show!"

These were the words the crowd was chanting as I sat in the Buckhorn Opera House, outside of Silver City, New Mexico, when I was fourteen or fifteen years old, dressed in fishnets that I had bought from Walmart in secret and two push-up bras overlapped on each other to make me look older.

I remember how the man at the front had eyed me suspiciously before ultimately drawing the V on my forehead in red lipstick. That night, all the hopelessness, despair, and soul-crushing loneliness that had plagued me like I was a haunted house in a young teenager's body lifted. I giggled as I went through my virgin sacrifice, a Rocky Horror tradition that is more silly than it sounds, I gasped as I saw the man who I believed was a conservative furniture store owner show his bare ass on stage in an open medical gown as Frank N. Furter, and most importantly, I felt a sense of belonging that I had never even dreamt of feeling, had never known was something my body and poorly handed heart could feel.

When a child is born, they are born as a soul that have never yet been caged to a body of flesh and bone.

A child fresh out of their mother's womb is wild, they are wired to explore, flourish, crawl, run, cry, scream, giggle, love. If that baby is a boy, he may be expected to be unruly, loud, rambunctious, and confident. He is born to a world where he is the King, and we all know the King sits higher than the Queen. If that baby is a girl, she may be expected to be soft-spoken, shy, subservient, helpful, caring. She is born to a world where she is less than and will have fewer rights to her own body as her male counterpart. We all know that a good girl is a quiet one.

A girl may find herself ruthlessly and unapologetically confined, yet the beautiful monster persists within her—the creature that prowls her heart and dreamscape, flexing its claws behind the iron bars, despite patriarchy's relentless attempts to drive them to extinction, refusing to vanish. Whether carefully concealed beneath a mask of people-pleasing and smiling through life's battles or lying dormant, even to the woman herself, the wild and formidable beast inside remains. Within all women, a monster lies.

When I was a little girl, I wanted to spend my time with the cows, the birds, and the water. Instead, I spent time sitting on the floor of my closet, desperate for enough quiet just to hear the sounds of my breaths hitting my upper lip.

In my twenty-sixth year of life, I am just now starting to get acquainted with the creature of desire, vibrancy, and the longing to belong that lurks under my flesh, but after years of hearing her disembodied roars and the uncomfortable but necessary experience of her trying to flex her talons after being restricted for so long, I am ready to let myself arch my back and bare my teeth and embody her. I would like, if I may, to take you on a journey, a strange and beautiful and horrible and fantastical journey, of the process of uncaging my gorgeous, ferocious, tender inner beast.

When I was no older than ten years old, I watched the 2005 American Girl movie, Felicity, and in the movie, Felicity rides a horse. After the movie was over, I snuck out to the barn and climbed onto the corral panels, then onto my father's quarterback named Shotgun. My father looked out the window and saw his shy and timid daughter and her tiny body with pajama bottoms on, perched bareback on a horse who had been named after his tendency to bolt from underneath his rider with no warning. I know he has been proud of me many times, but this was my first memory of the feeling of his pride. He was proud of my courage, not of my smallness.

As a little girl, I had the spark of wild that all children do when they are born. I wanted to wander the arroyos by our house, lay on my back on a bed of leaves at the river, climb trees and pretend to be on the lookout of a pirate ship, go hiking through the tall grasses next door and pretend I was Frodo with the ring on a trek to Mordor, and spend hours looking at the Milky Way. I was silly, creative, and strange.

Also as a little girl, I was taught that privacy was a privilege not afforded to me, that my body was not only mine, but was an extension of my mother's, a limb of hers that she claimed as soon as I was born, insisting that I should not be able to change with the door closed, because as she put it, we were just two girls. I learned quickly that in addition to being property of my mother, my body was also to be of service to men, and that what I didn't give willingly would inevitably be taken from me, consensually or otherwise. When you're afraid of being taken, sometimes you resort to giving it freely so that you can rewrite the narrative so that it is less unbearable to sit with as you try to go to sleep at night.

I knew that I was a strange child, one that once told her third grade class that her cat was her sister (which did not decrease the amount of strange and bewildered looks I got) because she felt so connected to the animal's sweet spirit and gentle heart, likely because it mirrored my own. I didn't embrace this sensitivity, I was ashamed by it, and was encouraged by the world around me to try and conform as much as possible to be a good, "normal" girl. Whatever wild part of me that my mother's abuse didn't tame, the patriarchy in action in others did. I learned to wear too-tight clothes that made boys and men stare at me in a way that made me know I had their approval, but made my bones feel rough with the feeling that a flower must feel after it's been picked and crammed in a vase only to die a few days later; my beauty and sexuality were all that mattered, and Goddess forbid that I owned that sexuality for myself. I was just like that flower, grabbed and mangled and on display. My body, my desires, my self was not for me, it was for others, and above all else: men.

My mother didn't model female friendships for me, she was isolated and distrusting of other women, and she raised me to be the same. I wasn't allowed to spend the night too often at my best friend's house, whose parents she had known for years, but I was able to spend the night at my boyfriend's house at only sixteen. This was because men were always to be trusted, and women were not even worth spending time with - a rather tender subject.

When I was twelve, I cried underneath my sacred Milky Way and the moon that felt more like God than the threatening male entity that the churches told me was god (why is it that only God can judge us, but men are always convicting women of sins that they committed?), because I knew that I wasn't straight, that I loved and had feeling for girls as well as boys, perhaps even more so, because I wasn't afraid of them or feel used by them. No women ogled me from their cars as I walked, yet we were positioned as the enemy of one another instead of the wild sisterhood that should have come naturally to us.

In her book, *Communion*, bell hooks says that "almost all of us are raised in homes that value and uphold patriarchal thinking." She went on to say that girls "must be good to be loved. And good is always defined by someone else, someone on the outside." All my life, there had always been one goal: above all, be good.

Be nice, be palatable, be quiet, be seen, and don't dare to be heard.

It was like being shattered. How could I appease the world we live in, the one that wants a girl to be smart, but not too smart, sweet, but not overly sweet, and pretty, but not so pretty that she knows she's pretty? How do I make my erratic, abusive mother happy, even though, in retrospect, she likely didn't know how to even experience true happiness. Everything I did, everything I said, everything I wore was wrong, on some level. My hair was too brown, too short, my teeth too yellow, eyebrows too bushy, oh, and did I gain weight?

In Ava Reid's novel, *Juniper and Thorn*, the main character, Marlinchen, says, "I would smile blithely if someone tried to saw off my leg. But no one ever told me I was allowed to scream." Later, the character states that "wanting anything ended only in misery." When I was a child, I don't remember wanting often. I know that I needed everything to just be okay. It didn't occur to me that no matter what I did, it likely wouldn't be.

When I was in college, I had never felt so simultaneously free while also so overwhelmed, feeling like I was drowning in the unprocessed trauma of my childhood that had engulfed me like a flash flood of unbridled pain. I slowly started to drink more and more, then more, and then a little more after that. I woke up with mind shattering headaches from drinking over the weekend, and during the week I fell asleep high out of my mind.

I remember one night, as I lay in my lofted bed that I shared with another girl (the sweetest and kindest girl, who thankfully stayed in my life despite me being such an absolute mess when she first met me), and I watched as the uneven ceiling started to close in on me. I was terrified, but then I reminded myself that it was just because I was high. This should have been alarming to me, should have perhaps been a sign that maybe I should smoke less. It wasn't.

The next morning, when it was hard to wake up, I put pineapple vodka in a disposable coffee cup when I woke up at six in the morning, and went to work with it.

Possibly the best part of my first year of college was the people that I met. I met some truly horrible people, and slept with some of them, too, but I had also met people who made me realize that I could be liked, even loved. When I was growing up, I had only one true friend, and she left when I was fourteen. I was alone, and to survive, I learned how to pretend to be someone I wasn't so that I could find a false sense of belonging.

Earlier, when I said I didn't want much growing up, I was wrong. What I wanted, above all else, was to belong.

If belonging feels like a balloon that grows inside your chest so large that it eventually pops and coats your insides with golden warm honey, false belonging feels like being stripped naked in a gray room with no windows, and then telling everyone that you're fine, thanks, you don't need anything, and smiling as you work for everyone's approval. That is to say, it feels empty, hollow, and painful, and the feeling of wanting haunts its victim, laughing at them because they will never, ever, achieve what they desire.

When you don't belong, all you can see are the ways that you can mold yourself, hide yourself, contour yourself into being what someone else wants you to be. At first, it doesn't feel so bad. It's easy! At the time I am writing this, there is a viral TikTok sound (although, by the time you're reading this, it could very well be banned, because even though our country can't agree on genocide, reproductive rights, whether Black Lives Matter, or if the Holocaust actually happened, there's one thing we can agree on, which is that an app that allows free speech and information sharing should be banned) that says, "Oh, you like my personality? Thanks, it's yours!"

That sound might be funny for a ten-second video, but when you're living it, the humor fades away. Masking when at special work events, or around hard to read family members is mostly harmless, but when you're masking so frequently, it feels like you're giving pieces of yourself away. No one can belong when there is nothing of them left.

In the book *Unmasking Autism*, Devon Price said, "Before I started unmasking, I felt cursed, and almost dead inside. Existence seemed like one long slog." I could relate. Suddenly, I knew what Dr. Scott meant when he had said, "And crawling, on the planet's face, some insects, called the human race. Lost in time, and lost in space... and meaning."

I had no meaning if my only goal was to belong to everyone, because it meant that I didn't belong to anyone.

Mara Glatzel, in her book *Needy*, states that "in an effort to belong to others, I had stopped belonging to myself." Well, I never had quite known who I was, had never truly belonged to myself to begin with, but when I saw Rocky Horror for the first time, I knew I was made from the same (likely very small, black, and tastefully lacy) cloth that the people around me were made out of.

If you don't know, or haven't seen it, The Rocky Horror Picture Show is a 1975 independent musical comedy horror film based on the 1973 musical stage production The Rocky Horror Show. Directed by Jim Sharman and featuring a cast led by Tim Curry, Susan Sarandon, and Barry Bostwick, it pays homage to science fiction and horror B movies from the early to mid-20th century. The plot revolves around a young engaged couple, Brad (asshole!) and Janet (slut!), whose car malfunctions near a castle during a storm. Seeking assistance, they encounter Dr. Frank N. Furter, a seemingly deranged scientist who introduces them to his creation, a living muscle man named Rocky. As the story unfolds, Frank's true identity is disclosed—he is an alien "transvestite" hailing from the planet Transsexual in the galaxy of Transylvania—and he seduces the couple into staying for a bite and a night, and true chaos follows.

While the language might be outdated, the film, and the live shadow cast productions, are still very much relevant. Despite facing a negative reception at first, The Rocky Horror Picture Show experienced a turnaround when it became a cult hit as a midnight movie at New York City's Waverly Theater in 1976. Viewers actively engaged with the film by returning to cinemas frequently, interacting with the screen, and even dressing up as characters, sparking the creation of numerous similar performance groups throughout the United States. As of now, it is the longest-running theatrical release in film history.

Even though the plot makes very little sense, one thing has held true for decades: Rocky Horror is a place to be weird, loud, expressive, and your unique self. When you're there, time is fleeting, and you're able to truly let madness take control.

In January of 2020, I felt like I was breaking.

Every day was a struggle to exist. I was getting to work at six thirty in the morning, doing a job that would help me get into a PhD program I was pretty sure I didn't want to do, but someone else (a man) told me I should, so I believed him. Despite having graduated with my Bachelors degree, I was still taking courses, because why not, my work paid for them, and it's what I thought I should do. After work, I would go out with my coworkers and drink a beer I didn't like, because I should do it, or I would go to the gym, because that's what I should do. I would go home and cook a keto friendly dinner, because, of course, I was willing to follow a diet where I could eat bacon and sour cream at every meal, but Goddess forbid I have a carrot that made me nearly shit myself every single day. I wanted to lose weight - why? Because I thought I should.

I was at my wits end, when my partner agreed to go see The Rocky Horror Picture Show in February 2020. I remember how it felt to get ready to make the forty-five-minute drive to Meow Wolf in Santa Fe to see my favorite show, although this one was unique, because it was entirely performed by a drag queen shadow cast, with Brad and Janet played by the same queen, half Brad and half Janet.

Painting on my red lips, and squeezing my breasts into a low, plunging cut black shirt - I didn't wear a single bra, much less two, oh how times had changed… except, they hadn't changed, not really. I wasn't much different than that fourteen - or was it fifteen - year-old girl. I may have not stuffed my bra anymore, and now I knew the words to Science Fiction Double Feature, and knew when to yell "slut!" at the screen, but I was still at my core, yearning for connection and safety.

For belonging.

Becca Piastrelli, in her book *Root and Ritual*, states that the craving for belonging is innate, saying that "like our ancestors, we wither without a tangible sense of intimate connection." She defines belonging as "'feeling at home,' where to be at home is to be seen and known."

When our world changed irrevocably and completely the following month, in March 2020, I was literally stuck at home. At first, it was like being trapped with a stranger. Have you ever seen *The Chilling Adventures of Sabrina*? If so, perhaps you can recall the scene where Nick traps Lucifer in his body as a flesh Acheron. If not, I am sure you can imagine how painful and gruesome it might feel to have such an internal battle raging inside of your body every moment of every day.

In many ways (though my own company is, I like to think, a bit nicer than the devil's), this is what those early months of the COVID-19 lockdown felt like. However, as time began to melt and ebb and stretch, and I knew I was stuck with myself, I began the most painful thing I have ever had to do: I began to get to know myself.

In 2022, a day after the ninth year anniversary of the most traumatic instances in my life (a sexual assault that had happened when I was fifteen years old), a day that always carried with it unwelcome flashbacks and spells of heartbreak and tears, I went by myself to The Rocky Horror Picture Show, in Albuquerque, New Mexico, hosted by Pride & Equality Magazine.

I had wanted to take my partner and go with friends, and I had gotten my ticket a month in advance, but by the time my friends tried to get theirs, it was sold out. At this time, I still shied away from doing anything by myself; I hated going to Target alone, much less put on my red feather boa and go to a midnight showing of a movie and yell at the screen and throw rice and playing cards by myself.

Eventually, I decided to go on my own. I had been trying to practice the art of doing things alone, even when it was hard. I was still on my journey of truly getting to know myself that I had been on since 2020. For those years, I experienced what bell hooks, in *Communion*, called the tear "between my desire to follow the dictates of my inner self and my distrust of that self."

I decided to trust my inner self.

When I left the theater late that night, or technically, it was the next morning, I lay next to my partner in bed and told him, "Next year, I will be in Rocky."

Beginning to know myself and integrate all of my broken pieces and jagged edges might have been the most painful thing I have ever done, but one of the scariest things must have been standing on the stage of The Guild theater, an uncomfortably bright spotlight in my face while I sang (did I mention that I can't sing?) a Mamas and Papas song urging strangers to dream a little dream of me.

I was cast as Janet Weiss, and every broken little piece of me sang.

In October 2023, on the day of my sexual assault anniversary, I stood on stage in front of a sold-out audience in my white bra and slip and lip-synced along to "Touch a Touch Me." If belonging felt like warm honey in my chest, then fulfilling a dream ten years in the making that represented embracing my bisexuality, my weirdness, my freedom, the life I had created free of abuse, performing in The Rocky Horror Picture Show, with my chosen family in the audience cheering me on with red Vs on the foreheads, felt like home.

I was home, both in myself and in the community I had carefully and intentionally created for myself.

The war between my contained demon and my true self had ended. Adrienne Rich said, "A thinking woman sleeps with monsters that beak which grips her, she becomes." Or, as Dr. Frank N. Furter said, "don't dream it, be it."

Even now, I find that it's not always easy having a good time. I have to push myself to enjoy the beautiful life I have. I have to remind myself of gratitude. I have to pull myself out of bed after losing sleep with puffy eyes. However, no matter how many traumas I have to process, no matter what I go through next, I remember this:

I'm a wild and an untamed thing.
I'm a bee with a deadly sting.

Michelle Renee

Michelle (she/her/they) was born and raised in the Gila Valley. She has always maintained a deeply rooted connection to nature, wildlife, and the innate wildness that exists deep within the human core, that constant call of feral awakening. She began playing piano at the age of three to assuage the loneliness of being the youngest of eight, when all other siblings went to school, and expanded that passion to include dance, writing, art, and all things creative.

Michelle currently resides in southwestern New Mexico, near her parents, Roy and Judie, continuing her inquiry of all Divine symbiotic relationships. She has two beautiful children, Layla and Jake, who are the loves of her life, and spends her time snuggling her spunky pup, Cootay, admiring the fierce and lovable Marry Potter, (her cat that happens to have a perfect lightning bolt on her forehead), composing music, drawing, painting, reading, writing, exploring outdoors, rockhounding and living in rhythm with the Moon.

Heart's Rewilding

The sky has turned to velvet,
Reminds me of your voice...
A taste of chocolate cherry
In the back of your Rolls Royce.
The colors of the skyline,
You bit my lip so sweet -
In the dead of winter,
But all I feel is heat.
The way your eyes undo me,
There's fire in your smile.
Accelerant in human form,
You strike a match in style.
Fingertips that take road trips,
Back roads to explore...
Hike along the ridge line
Till you're begging me for more.
Oh, I better stop right there.
My thoughts have been too bold.
I'll think of you another day
To warm me from the cold.

Michelle Renee
July 22, 2024

Just One Spark

Undo my button... Undo my snap.
Undo the harness of this mental trap.
Undo the brokenness. Undo the shame.
Time to be bold, my dear.
Time to reclaim.

Undo the fears, and Unlearn the guilt.
These are just tactics society built.
Stand in your power. Stand in your light!
This is our Humanness. This is our right!

Do not twist, contort, or break
to be a part of something fake.
Belonging isn't fitting in.
It's acceptance in your truest skin.

Do not fear the dark, my love.
Stars will guide from up above.
Should the fear begin to sneak,
listen to these words I speak;

If you find you're in the dark,
remember, it takes only one spark...
Just one candle flicker, friend, and
You have caused the
Dark the end.

Michelle Renee
July 7, 2024

Perspective Altered

The very vine that had fed her,
nurtured her into being, wrapped tighter...
Perspective altered,
as the soil hardened,
the harsh breath of summer
a stark contrast from the internal cold -
the external source, a suffocation.
As mystery often does,
it unraveled,
and the softening arrived.
The gentle whisper of hope took root,
and again, the nurturer returned,
weeping her relief... a salty welcome,
tempered by gentle waves of loving connection;
Perspective altered, as the soil palliated,
holding her in its firm embrace.
She grew, a wildflower,
dancing to the melody of the sun,
swaying to the magnificence of the stars,
confiding in her friend,
the moon.
Fresh petals, exposed...
tiny leaves of curiosity, uncurling, extending,
tasting the rain...
Perspective altered, as the soil grew rich...
germinating dreams, friendship, adventure,
love...

Captivated, enticed by the horizon
and all the blossoms that grew
lush beyond the tree line,
a tender obsession of things to come...
When a spark, at first fascinating,
beautiful and unexpected, exploded,
torching petals to ash...
Perspective altered, eroding the landscape of her
heart, soil, hydrophobic, a protection from the
pain.
Night fell, and she rested - worn, ragged,
wounded...
until finally, the nurturer again returned,
calling her to rise, gently, slowly,
humming her loving song...
awakening the sparrow within her forest of
ambition...
planting fresh seeds in a soil,
lavish with wisdom, empathy, light...
the roots healing, her mind reseeding,
and the garden returned, even more splendid,
more alluring... a vast paradise;
Perspective altered.

Michelle Renee
July 22, 2024

And I Wondered

A laugh, a sigh and the way
she bit her bottom lip with
nervous anticipation,
while I watched sparks flicker across
eyes the color of sunlight through
sap in an evergreen forest,
and I wondered.

Perhaps I was mistaken.
Perhaps I had misread her landscape.
Perhaps my heart was incompatible
with the depths of the oceans
she created with the gentle caress
of her hand, swallowing me up in the
hypnotic glow of her soul,
igniting my skin, pulse accelerated,
and I wondered.

An invitation into a velveteen night,
where the heat of our breath mingled,
swirling like the butterflies in my stomach,
as her sweetness, delicately stated,
danced inside my mind.

A laugh, a sigh, as I
bit my bottom lip in
fevered anticipation while

sparks erupted across
eyes the color of honey in a
meadow of four leaf clovers,
and I wondered.

Perhaps I was astonished.
Perhaps we found common ground.
Perhaps my courage was compatible
with the demons that haunted her night,
an insistent longing to vanquish the
nightmares that gripped her
in her sleep...

a tendril of empathy,
binding us in an unspoken oath;
Together we would transmute
monsters to dust, banish them to the void,
and I wondered.

The world vanished.
The soft urgency of her lips,
the enticing taste of her tongue,
I melted, mesmerized by the
grip of her hands, the
sound of her breath...
and I wondered.

Perhaps this was the Divine pinnacle.
Perhaps I was enchanted.
Perhaps this is where Heaven meets Earth,

and the fire that consumes me with
every kiss, every touch, is a
reawakening after decades of exile,
my soul's renewal, the desert monsoon
after a lifetime of impervious suffocation,
recovery, transformation,
the returning to self,
and I wondered.

Michelle Renee
August 10, 2024

SAMANTHA NAGEL

You Belong

Hair too curly, limbs too spindly,
skin too pale, with freckles too.
Hear the laughter, feel the flush
creep in my cheeks, embarrassed hue.

Make me smaller, in the corner.
Hide the light. Don't snuff it out.
See me now. We hit fast forward,
combat boots, immense self doubt.

Powered by determination,
grit fed by illusive dreams,
stubborn will, anticipation,
pulling threads from tattered seams.

Lost in liquor, ecstasy,
mirrored in a stranger's eyes,
seeking all I longed to be,
scattered soul, now traumatized.

One, now three, now two, unite,
Run through fire. Run through hell.
Walk on eggshells, fight or flight,
angel on a carousel.

With her footing now regained,
wings realized and freedom claimed,
storms left hooks of shadows past,

haunting sleep, terrors cast.

Ivories offered soul's reprieve,
daytime drift through sleepy seas.
Tiny feet and tiny hands,
giggles, snuggles, Sweetheartland.

But still without external guide,
guilt and fear would soon reside.
Trained to seek outside myself,
hopes and needs went on the shelf.

Mirage exposed, view reframed,
a second angel took his name.
Poison bled. Joys turned to fears,
lotus babes with raven tears.

Scars from fault lines, cracked and flared,
harm too deep to be repaired.
Break the chain links. Come undone.
Four become three
Become two
Become
One.

Sitting silent, blue eyes closed,
hear the river as it flows.
Listen to the rippling breeze,
whisper through elm and

cottonwood leaves,

"You are the stars. You are the trees,
the birds, the air, the flowers, the bees.
You and I, we breathe as one,
from worm to wood to cloud to sun.
Rest your mind. Renew your heart.
Sunrise brings a hopeful start.
You are safe. You are strong.
All is well, and You belong."

Michelle Renee
08/10/2024

I Remember

Tiny silken thread, strobing in the morning air,
delightful; a private disco party for
an eight legged dancer.

Key lime tinted chlorophyll
absorbs the high point,
composing a decadent relief
from the scorching rays.

The wise ones, emanating
rest and magnificence,
cast long comforting arms
that enfold me.

Mother Gaia, her sweet confections
adorning,shimmer and sway to the harmonic
"chatter...chirp... warble... caw..."
the abiding flow of sparkling water
rounding out nature's band,
the stones and sand
a percussive hush,
a lullaby for the weary mind.

Insects swirl above the surface like live confetti,
and tadpoles dart beneath the glittering ripples,
an organic disco lava floor, but better.

SAMANTHA NAGEL

The earth still damp from the
night's cosmic drum circle,
the evening's grand finale
an enchanting display of lights
as electricity flashed,
swift and mesmerizing across
charcoal and sapphire thunderheads,
a Divine rave of the Highest order,
And I, a VIP at the most exclusive club.

I come to feel whole,
to calm the thoughts
that race persistently...
a personal 24 Hours of Le Mans,
And Oyster is on the menu.

As I perch upon a fallen deadwood,
supported by its enduring strength,
cradled by its softness even as it decays
slowly back to its beginnings,
They remind me...

"You are no visitor here, but instead
a silken thread all your own,
strobing in the morning air,
delightful; a private disco party
infused with a two legged dancer...
a walking, breathing,
living being;
a Divine rave of

the Highest order."

And I remember,
I am whole.

Michelle Renee
August 12, 2024

Kayleen Schenk

Kayleen (they/she) is a theatre lover, fur baby parent, super-in-love partner and sometimes fantasy writer. They grew up reading books in trees until it was nearly too dark to climb down and now spends their adult days striving to write words worth reading up in the leaves and branches.

Living in and growing up around New Mexico has played a huge role in their creative journey. Their theatre studies and performances have taken them around the world, from the neon funland of Las Vegas, Nevada to the historic cobblestones of Paris, France. But the high desert forests of Southeastern New Mexico have always called her home. Welcoming her with open arms (and the best weather).

Kayleen's writing interests are a colorful pool of sci-fi, fantasy and wild epics. Their favorite stories growing up were the Earth's Children series and Jurassic Park; stories where the line between civil and wild are blurred, sometimes ending in joy, other times in terror and doom. One of the best lessons these stories have taught them is that it is up to humans how things play out: respect the wild and you will most often find joy. Disrespect equals the aforementioned terror and doom.

Kayleen can usually be found sipping tea with their partner on the back porch of their home, surrounded by many dogs, chickens and a fluffy kitty named Pigeon.

Noble & Wicked Beasts

If you're hunting for a saga, a fairytale, a legend! Then you've wandered into the right den. Take it from an old fox, albeit one with a penchant for embellishment, the stories of The Realm are a splendid tapestry of species coexisting within their designated territories. Picture this: graceful elk who stride through the forests with the air of royalty, sleek bobcats who prowl through the underbrush with elegance, fast as the Roaring River. And horned owls who, with their timeless wisdom, could probably solve all the world's problems if only they cared to stay awake long enough. Then there's us, the foxes—clever and mischievous, with a touch of finesse that the more pompous among us often overlook.

Magic here isn't some abstract concept or a mere trinket to be waved about. It's a living essence, flowing through our land like a lifeblood. It sparkles in the morning dew, shimmers in the riverspray, and hums through the veins of every noble beast who calls this place home. You see, this magic doesn't belong to any one species. It belongs to the land itself, to all of us who cherish it and live in harmony with it.

But we didn't always know that. Some of us still don't.

As with any grand tale, peace is a fleeting luxury. Not all creatures within The Realm are as noble as they might seem. Some, with hearts darker than a raven's wing, believe magic is their divine right, a sign of their superiority. They twist it and turn it, cleaving the very fabric of peace apart to satisfy their own selfish ambitions.

Enter the Western Wolves. Ah, yes, the wolves. A cunning lot, with a ruler so ambitious that even I, in my cynical old age, have to admire their audacity. For fifteen years, they harbored a belief so profound it's almost laughable: their lightning, their so-called supremacy, entitles them to be the apex predators of The Realm. In their grand delusion, they decided that every other creature is lesser, unworthy of the magic that courses through our lands.

And so, they struck. Lightning cracked through The Realm, once, twice—like a cosmic exclamation point to their self-righteous claims. The first bolt set in motion a series of wild events: the murder of a king, the toxic grief of a queen, lords and ladies battling to protect their people, feathered and furred alike . It tore through the peace and turned our world into a theater of conflict and intrigue. The second bolt? Oh, that's the real gristle in the teeth! Lighting paths that led many of us to rediscover things thought lost forever. Within the lands and within ourselves.

So, settle in. If you've a mind for adventures, vengeance, and a bit of magic-touched mayhem, you're in for a tale that's far from predictable. Just remember, that even in a world where lightning strikes twice, a fox's wit can be the most potent magic of all.

Waves, white-capped and frigid, broke against the bow of an ancient ship of black wood. The carved, howling wolf on its prow showed the damage of numerous past battles, yet it still cut through the water. A formidable force of doom spelt out plainly for the inhabitants of the growing shore in a language of conquest and magic.

The Wolves of the West would not be greeted with peace and hospitality when they arrived in port.

For it was because of their magic; their scheming tactics of espionage and coup twelve years past that had caused the former late King of the bay they now fervently sailed through to die an excruciatingly painful death. A regicide so traumatic, the widow-queen outlawed magic of any kind in grief and disgust.

Her trauma was a living thing through the land. Scented by Lupé Allsfoot on the seaspray misting his muzzle and in the breeze that flapped the ship's sails. Tangy and bitter all at once, leaving him scrunching his muzzle and fighting the urge to shake his great furry head free of the acrid stench.

Western Wolves do not balk, do not break. It is with clawed magic and cunning that we take, Lupé recited silently to himself.

The Wolves of the West would soon be ashore. The Antler Castle looming closer with every stroke of the oars, growing like an angry with the promise of conflict and seething with hate for the lupine banners progressing through the waters.

Lupé cast his eyes to the red and black sails of the Western Wolves and across the deck to his fellow canines-in-arms and felt a shiver run up his spine. He was only newly named Beta of the Fleet. An honor of daunting proportions that grew more heavy on his chest as they drew closer to the pale gray sands.

He wondered if they would soon be soaked red and let up a howl from deep within his belly for the wolves whose blood stained the beaches between here and Loberia: their far away, forested homelands on the western islands.

Regardless of how the Court of Antler and Horn - led by the widowed elk Queen Alcene - chose to meet their most hated foe on the sands ahead, Lupé knew this would be the last time he saw all of his canines-in-arms, his pack, gathered as one, rowing through the cold fog of enemy waters. Ready to bring their hated magic back to these lands by any means necessary.

For it was certain that battles of magic and might loomed just ahead, conflicts more than a decade in the making teeming to be settled with powers forged with steel and antler, against those of spells and mystery.

Twelve years earlier…

"Diego! Diego, stop pulling my tail!" Rang out the little bobcat cub's voice. A tangle of paws and spots barreled around the warmly-lit den, punctuated by youthful yowls and innocent hisses. The Prides kept no servants, everyone pulling weight for mealtimes and cub rearing, royal children scrapping and learning alongside cubs from adjoining dens. Even in Lady Mara and Lord Mateo's royal lodgings.

"I am Lord of Dinner! Hear me roar!" The largest cub, the tail-puller Diego, proclaimed from atop the table.

A majestic, large female bobcat strode into the den clad in a burgundy velvet cape. The brooch fastening the garment the likeness of a golden salmon, mouth agape and scales polished to perfection. The female's sharp eyes left no room for nonsense as she took in the sight of her son standing atop the dining table.

The cub, all of the cubs in fact, halted in the Lady's presence. Their ruckus and shenanigans frozen under Her Majesty's icy gaze. As if she were leveling justice on a criminal amongst the Prides, as if she would strike their breast with her sharp claws and cast them in the torrid river; the traditional punishment for those who found themselves guilty in Riverclaw territory.

But her sharp, golden eyes melted. Her whiskers twitching in humor. She sketched a theatrically low bow to her son and asked, "Does this Lady have permission to announce the beginning of the Feast, Lord of Dinner? I'm sure the gathered Prides are getting hungry above."

Diego, ever playful and mischievous, made a show of contemplating his answer.

"Hmmmm," he responded. Scratching his fuzzy white chin with a tiny claw. "You may, mother...I mean, Lady Mara. Let the Feast of the Prides begin!"

"Thank you, kind Lord. Now hop off that table and help the other cubs bring out the goblets."

Lady Mara Riverclaw followed the cubs laden with goblets of water and mulled wine up into the vast autumnal clearing where Prides of all kinds were gathered. In the heart of the lush wilderness, nestled between towering pines and a roaring river, lay her own family's territory. To her left, her brother Lord Mateo spoke with the short, powerful leader of the coastal Prides. Her young daughter Dani, future co-leader of the Riverclws, was helping the pale-furred cubs from the Mountaintop Prides disperse goblets evenly amongst the divinely decorated tables.

For generations, these majestic creatures ruled this vast expanse of The Realm with a regal demeanor, their pelts adorned with patterns that bespoke a lineage of strength and nobility. The Riverclaws were known far and wide for their unity and prowess in defending bobcat territory - mountaintop to coast - against any threat that endangered their people and other creatures they protected.

Lady Mara locked eyes with her brother and gave a small nod, suggesting he find his preferred seat at the high table. She scanned the crowds of spotted felines to where she knew she would find her mate, Stephan, delighting a group of friends and strangers alike with his booming voice and charming jokes. He towered over every other cat near him, his broad shoulders impressively built from rowing their traditional vessels up and down the powerful river. As the pride's Captain of the River, he was charged with all of their nautical affairs. From fishing to exploration, vessel construction to repairs, Stephen knew the Roaring River that defined bobcat borders and livelihoods better than nearly any cat present.

As she met his gaze, Stephan's humorous eyes heated and his smile widened. He dismissed himself from the thick crowd still laughing from his cajoling and joined her side, ever the content consort ready to support her. She reached for his strong paw and gave a loving and grateful squeeze. The Lady cleared her throat and called out in a clear and commanding voice, "Please, all! Find your seats amongst friends, old and new. Mix the Prides! Let us feast!"

As the sun dipped below the horizon, casting an amber glow across the festivities, all cats were settled in their seats and ready to dine. Coastal cats were seated by felines from the thick forests and woods. Mountain dwellers shared wine with plains cats and admired the trees decorated with fragrant herbs and garland surrounding the clearing. All of the excitement was scored by the roaring of the river. Lady Mara and Lord Mateo shared a grateful look at what they had accomplished in gathering everyone here at the Royal Den.

Once a silence filled the air and all looked to the high table for the feast's opening speech, Stephan grasped his goblet confidently in his giant paw and rose.

"Welcome all to this joyous night! It fills me with happiness to see everyone under the same sunset, celebrating the vast territory and collaborative peace we strive so hard for as bobcats."

He placed his free paw on Mara's shoulder and squeezed. "Of course, none of this would be possible without leadership characterized by wisdom and benevolence. Qualities that not only endear but command respect. Let us raise our goblets to Lady Mara and Lord Mateo, the greatest co-rulers the Riverclaws have seen in several ages. Your mother and uncle were good to us all. Taught you well, but to unite the Prides is a mark of great power. Thank you for being the formidable duo that uphold the values of the bobcat. To the Lady and Lord!" Stephan ended with a proud raise of his glass.

"To the Lady and Lord," the clearing rang out. Followed by a chorus of yowls and chatterings and roars from maws young and old.

"Now! Eat, you animals!" Shouted the Lady's consort to hearty laughs and whoops. And all at once several dozen bobcats began to tear into glistening roasts, guzzling gallons of mulled wine and rich river water. The sounds gave hint to the wild capabilities of the humane people gathered. That once they were not as they are now, clothed in finery and dining in decorated splendor, but perhaps were once primordial creatures that summoned fear to their enemies instead of sharing peace with friends.

"Diego! I said, *no tail pulling*!" Dani shouted from the end of the royal table, swatting her twin brother with small but swift claws. Her spotted face crinkled in anger as she made to pounce from her seat.

"Dani!" Mara called. "You both may spar when the tables have cleared, but now…"

Mara paused.

As had Stephan, mid-joke. And Mateo as he chewed a roasted wing of meat.

Nothing seemed to change, but a sharp unease had run through the adults of the royal table, their keen feline senses attuned to any disturbances in their lands.

The unease seemed to be spreading, adding a sharp tang of confusion to the clearing as fur-tufted ears swiveled for clues to any impending threats. Whiskers twitched like hundreds of quivering pine needles.

A frantic crashing sounded from the north and every pair of eyes and ears craned towards the thick wood. The growing crashes were neither stealthy and calculated nor innocent and curious. They were frantic. And headed straight for the feast.

Suddenly a small deer leapt into the midst of gathered tables. Gasping for air and large eyes going ever wider as he took in the amount of felines bedecked in teeth and claws surrounding him. His left antler was snapped off nearly at the base, and the royal blue ribbons that adorned the royal court of Antler and Horn hung in tatters around his face. What struck the gathering most though, is that he was on All Fours: a stance or gait only used in times of significant feelings of excitement, fear, anger and lust. A position for ending and creating life. Or for fleeing death.

Lady Mara and Lord Mateo rose swiftly and crossed the clearing, Staphan and the twins following behind. At the sight of the large bobcats approaching the deer began to shiver. Mara raised her paws to show she meant no harm, seeing out of her sharp periphery that Mateo had done the same.

Her brother spoke softly as they continued their approach, "You are in no danger here. This is a place of peace." The deer's trembling softened, yet all four hooves remained on the ground.

"My brother speaks the truth. I see you wear the colors of King Barba and Queen Alcene's court. Are you a messenger?" Mara inquired.

At the mention of the elk King Barba, the deer seemed to wince. He bowed his head and began to sob. His outbreak had all of the bobcats glancing at one another in further unease.

In a trembling voice, the stag whispered, "Yes. I am Benmir. A messenger for… their majesties." Another sob.

"Easy, my friend," Mara spoke soothingly to the deer, her velvety cloak billowing in the tension-laden breeze. "Calm yourself and tell us your message."

Her assertive tone seemed to sober the stag, Benmir. He leveled his dark, round eyes - still brimmed with tears and fear - to her own gold ones, and delivered his news.

"King Barba, ruler of the Kingdom of Antler and Horn, is dead."

A wave of gasps flooded the gathered guests. But Benmir was not finished.

"Two nights past, the Western Wolves staged a coup while they dined as guests under His Majesty's roof. The feast thrown for our annual celebration of Shed-vaal. They…they poisoned him with their evil magic. He did not die quickly. Then they attacked the throne room with white lightning. Her majesty, Queen Alcene ordered any gathered Antler and Horn warriors to attack and detain all wolves who did not flee, but the wolves were ready with their tricks. They had the throne room surrounded, and incapacitated our forces and fled on their ships. Many warriors fell or are still in the burning clutches of the wolves' lightning tethers. Unable to move. Their fur and feathers singeing." Benmir stopped with a wince and several more silent tears.

Mara could not imagine being bound by burning lightning. Helpless to fight or aid her people as her abusers murdered her court members or fled. Her heart ached for the elk queen. Not just as a fellow ruler and warrior, but as a mate and a mother.

Stephan sensed Mara's shock and stepped forward to speak in her stead. "Our deepest sympathies for you and your court. But I must ask a frank question: If King Barba is dead and the wolves have fled, why has Her Majesty sent you in such haste? Why not keep every warrior close and send an owl or lesser bird with this message?"

Benmir continued, "Because the Wolves do not sail west back across the sea. They sail south, down the Roaring River…"

No, thought Mara. She interrupted him, "And straight for us."

Dread, pure and fast-growing dread filled the Lady, and from the sharp stench of fear now permeating the meadow, she guessed each bobcat present felt the same lead in their stomach.

Panicked shouts to flee and half-plans to fight sprang up at once.

"Prepare for defense!" Mara's voice cut through the chaos as she shouted specific orders to her trusted allies. Mateo, her twin and co-ruler, swiftly organized evacuation plans for the young, old and frail. Stephan sprinted to the Roaring River, shouting with a naval commander's call for bobcat warriors to join him. And they did. Mara watched as oarsmen and fighters from all Prides raced after her mate towards the river where they would use their vessels to block passage for the wolves.

Diego and Dani were given crucial tasks to ensure the safety of their fellow cubs within the tunnels of the Royal Den. She held their tiny faces between her paws and licked their brows. "You know the secrets. You know the twists and turns. Go, and I will find you." The twins looked at each other in the way they did before a race, but knew this was certainly no game, and ran, calling to the other cubs with small yips and yowls.

Other members of the Prides rallied, their faces reflecting a mix of fear and determination. Parents embraced cubs before their little legs raced after Dani and Diego. Claws were revealed at full length, daggers were pulled from sheaths beneath festive cloaks. Lady Mara watched the Royal Den's clearing transform from a calm sea of civil felines to an impressive expanse of bobcat warriors as fur rose along every spine and most front paws lowered to the earth.

Unsheathing her own claws, she turned back to the messenger who began quivering anew at the bobcat's poised for battle. "How much time do we have before the wolves arrive?" She asked.

The deer's response was swift and foreboding. "Not much, Your Majesty. The wolves are relentless, fueled by dark magic. They will be upon you before…."

A howl pierced the night. In its reverb was the promise of death and blood, spilt with crackling magic and a relentless quest to conquer and destroy.

Diego looked down at his rucksack, smartly packed with the essentials he would need for his journey, but surprisingly light as he considered the weight of his heart.

His grief. His anger.

Twelve years had not been enough to quell the tug of revenge in his chest. He was pretty sure the force would yank him right off his paws some days. Growing steadily stronger every moment since that dreaded howl had pierced the Gathering of the Prides. The last time any of the Prides had been together in one place.

A worn piece of gold was grasped in his paw. Nearly undefinable as a sacred salmon brooch that once fastened his mother's cloak. He squeezed his eyes shut and brought the keepsake to his lips - a common practice of his these last twelve years - before fastening it to the worn leather rucksack.

As Diego donned the pack and fastened his own green cloak about his broad shoulders, wandering footsteps shuffled behind him. The shuffling paused.

"All packed up and ready for his adventures…" a feathery voice whispered.

Diego turned. His uncle, Lord Mateo, was once a tall, charming figure. With a clear and kind voice capable of diplomacy and calming any dispute. Now he stood rather stooped. Formerly clear eyes, mirror images of Lady Mara's, were now a milky gold shadowed with demons. Were they the same demons that stirred in Diego's chest? Seeming to pull him across lands far from here, towards, he would swear by the River, the enemies he so wished to vanquish for stealing his family from him.

He rubbed at his chest, begging the pull to ease. *Soon*, he thought. *I will be off soon.*

"Yes, Uncle." Diego responded softly, reaching out his strong paw to grasp Mateo's thin arm, leading the quietly muttering male from the den and out into the warm summer morning.

The frail former co-leader gently sunk his claws into Diego's fur and whispered in a sing-song voice, "you know the secrets. You know the twists and turns. Go, and I will find you."

Mateo's chest tightened. His mother's last words to him.

He gave his uncle a tight smile, which was returned with a breathy laugh. Diego gave Lord Mateo's paw a final squeeze and gently nudged him into the sunshine before turning back to the Royal Den for the last time.

His mother's voice was a sweet caress in his mind. *You know the secrets. You know the twists and turns. Go, and I will find you.* With a map of The Realm in his pack, he certainly did know the twists and turns that would lead him to the Isle of the Western Wolves. There, he may not find his mother. His sister. But he would find his vengeance. And after that, maybe he would find some peace.

Diego slowly pivoted, his eyes scanning the familiar surroundings that had cradled his existence. The meadow, once a haven of joy and familial warmth winding through the aspens and pines, the strength of his people a living energy that enhanced the beauty around them, now seemed stale with his loss and grief. His family believed he was embarking on this journey to explore the world, to heal from the traumas that haunted his past. Little did they know, Diego's true motive was a vengeful quest he may never return from. A truth he had already come to terms with.

The meadow's lush grass, bathed in the soft glow of sunlight filtering through the aspen leaves, seemed to whisper memories of happier times. However, the pull in Diego's heart seemed to grow a consciousness. *Leave now,* it whispered desperately. Despite the urgency, he hesitated. Torn between the desire to escape without a word and the haunting beauty of the meadow that was all he had ever known.

I know. It is home. But leave now. The whispers urged.

Diego beat on his chest as if to clear his airways. To any bobcats passing by, he appeared to have coughed or choked on water. *The voice is growing impatient.* Diego chalked it up to his own excitement building. Eager to hit the trail and start his quest.

In the distance Diego observed Stephan, his late mother's mate, instructing the next set of twins destined to rule the Riverclaw Pride. The young bobcats were engaged in net weaving for fishing the river, a skill passed down through generations. He closed his eyes. He could hear the Roaring River. The laughter that had returned after the trauma of the Western Wolves' attack. Banal sounds of home that may one day refresh the Riverclaw territory. For all its staleness, he would miss this place once the road grew tough.

As he turned to leave, he found himself face-to-face with Stephan. *By the River! He was still quick.* Diego shot a look over his shoulder to see the twin cubs weaving alone. He returned his gaze rather sheepishly to the older male. Although his fur had whitened with age, spots fading from inky black to muted gray, Stephan stood strong and formidable. A captain through and through. Leader of a restored fleet that now graced the river's shores. The new head ship, Lady Mara, and a smaller, quicker vessel named The Dani, rocked gently in the current. Diego avoided laying eyes on his mother and sister's names emblazoned on the bows. The script was written with great care and artistry, contrasting with his final memories of the two females. A mixture of confusion and screaming and the crack of lightning cleaving his world in two.

Diego met Stephan's no-nonsense stare. "Off without a goodbye, boy?"

Diego shifted on his paws. "I…I didn't want to interrupt the twins' lesson. Their training is important."

"Yes." Staphen stated plainly. "Their training is paramount. But so are you. And I am happy you are going on this journey. Your mother and sister are gone. We have all found solace and a way to honor their memory through our service to the pride. But you, Diego, your solace lies beyond the Riverclaw territory, doesn't it?"

Stephan paused. An air of suggestion lay heavily between them. Diego averted his gaze. He could never lie to Stephan, his mother's strong mate. With the eyes of a captain, he missed nothing. Diego shifted on his paws again, whiskers twitching nervously.

Stephan smiled tightly and muttered, "Yes. Quite far, I'd wager." The male revealed a parcel from under his sea-green cloak. It was slender and rectangular, wrapped in worn leather, bound by the twine used in the fishing nets. He placed it gently in Diego's paws.

"Open it," the male directed. "I have a feeling you'll need it for your…adventures. Whatever they may be."

Diego tentatively unbound the twine, the leather wrappings falling open to reveal a simple, shining dagger. It's blade short but wicked sharp. The hilt fashioned with the pattern of salmon scales. He gripped the hilt in his paw, the tug in his chest giving a mighty heave.

"I had the blacksmiths of the mining Prides fashion it when you announced your journey this winter. Sailed further upstream to get it myself on last week's northern patrol. They weren't too keen to see a Riverclaw, with tension remaining between the Prides. But gold is gold. And they didn't turn down my handsome payment."

"Thank you, Stephan. It's…," Diego wondered if Stephan knew what kind of trouble Diego's quests may get him in. Preparing his late love's son the best he could without overstepping what Diego felt he needed to do. Even risking visiting other Prides while distrust and fear stained their alliances. "It…it will serve me well."

"I have no doubt about that. Keep it close." The Captain all of a sudden embraced Diego in a swift, crushing hug. "River guide you, son. We will be here upon your return. Whenever the currents lead you back."

He released Diego with misty eyes and a curt nod. Stepping aside, his large frame acting as a symbolic doorway swinging wide for Diego to step through. The young bobcat twitched his whiskers one last time, and set forth onto the road that held the promise of vengeance for his family and rest for his anxious heart.

In all of his plans for grand revenge, he had not accounted for the blisters, mosquitos, and splinters that stood between him and the Western Isles. Diego had the large, strong stature of a bobcat prince, spending every day training in physical activities befit wild royalty. He could wield a dagger, sail a ship, hunt lesser creatures and brawl in tournaments. But he quickly realized as he left the serenity of Riverclaw territory behind, the Roaring River's call fading with every mile, that he was - in fact - a prince.

A spoiled prince.

Although he would never take a crown and rule his people, for Riverclaws only ever co-ruled along with their twin. Once Dani was slain, his future as a ruler was wiped away, but he would always hold the monecor of Prince. If only in title and to show respect to the leadership of his mother and uncle.

But he only ever ran as far as it took to capture prey. Only parried with swords long enough to disarm other trainees. Only shouted orders to other bobcats when sailing the riverways. At the early burn of yet another blister forming on his toe pads, he realized that those other trainees must have let him win because of who his mother was. Who he and his sister were to become.

Spoiled rotten.

It was only sundown of his first day on the trail and he was already feeling strain and shortcomings. As he crested a small hill near the base of the Snow Capped Mountains, the landmark he was to follow for the first leg on his journey, the sun was transitioning from its play of colors across the clouds towards the grays and blues of dusk.

His breath was a sawing in his chest and a conspicuous exertion amongst the peaceful wild around him.

A raspy, heckling call burst from above his head. "Oy! The sunset ain't *that* breathtaking, kitty. Get a grip."

Sill gasping for air, Diego squinted his eyes to search for the source of the cajoling. He brought his paw up to block the sun's final rays blinding his eyes.

The voice sounded again from behind him. "Over here, kitty."

Diego whirled, spotting a scruffy black crow perched on a branch a few feet above him. It's dark eyes squinted in laughter as it grabbed the trunk of the tree with one wing, the other going to its breast. It opened its beak and proceeded to let out an imitation of Diego's labored breathing.

Diego was not impressed. His tail twitched with embarrassment. He hollered at the crow, "you pest! How long have you been stalking me?"

"Ha! Stalk? No need to stalk. The whole of the wood heard ya coming for miles. I perched on a branch nearby and waited oh so hopefully. I thought ya might be perishin', from the sound of that pantin'. Dinner time! I thought. But alas. Here ya are. Alive and…well, let's just say alive."

This was the last thing Diego needed. Another blow to his pride. "Well, off with you, then. You're not wanted here."

"Not wanted? Oh! My poor, gentle heart, kitty! Ya wound me." The crow let out another raspy laugh, clicking its beak at Diego. "No one wants me around. But I'm around. I'm circlin' and seein' more than you ever will."

"My name isn't Kitty, bird. It's Diego Riverclaw. I'm honorary prince and former ruler-to-be of the Riverclaw Pride." Diego puffed out his chest and stood a little taller, expecting the declaration to wipe the smug look off the bird's beak.

"Ah! A fancy kitty, then." The crow replied.

Diego hissed, "I'm not a kitty. I'm a bobcat. And a fancy…I mean… royal bobcat, at that."

A snort and another click from the bird. "You're all kitties from the skies. Little specks of fluff prowlin about with yer pride and purrs. Don't make no difference to Chauncy."

"To who?" Diego asked.

"Chauncy! That's me. Ol' Chauncy the Crow. Oldest crow in this here valley."

"More like *loudest* crow in this here valley," Diego muttered.

"What was that, kitty?"

"Nothing, crow. Just…just be off now. I'm on an important journey and I don't need pesky birds like you squawking after me." With a decided huff Diego turned on clawed feet and strode off, ignoring the cramping in his legs from climbing the hill. He couldn't give the crow the satisfaction of seeing him limp.

"All right, Kitty. Limp away now. Ol' Chauncy's gonna enjoy the sunset. I'll catch up with ya in no time," the crow hollered from behind.

Diego yelled without looking back, "just leave me alone, bird!"

He hunched his spotted shoulders and quickened his pace. *Best to get rid of this nuisance before dark*, Deigo thought. *I'll make camp once the first stars appear.*

The incessant bird did - in fact - catch up to Diego in no time. The bobcat was setting up his small camp under the pale glittering of dusk's first stars. Glad to have evaded the annoying crow and feeling good and tired - albeit a little humbled - after his first day of journeying.

He was striking flint together over a bundle of dried twigs and fibers when an unmistakable *fwoop fwoop fwoop* of sturdy wings sounded in the branches above, followed by the *click click* of a beak.

Diego froze. *Please don't be the crow. Please don't be the crow*, he muttered in his mind.

"Kitty!"

"Ggggrrrr!" Diego growled, whiskers twitching erratically. He refused to look up and continued to strike the flint more aggressively.

"Good thing Ol' Chauncy's here. Gotta have a lullaby before ya lay yer head down for a cat nap," Chancy said.

"If you sing one note Feather Brain it will be the last thing you ever do," Diego uttered menacingly.

"Gonna climb up here and give me a taste o' them claws, ay Kitty?"

"No," Diego whispered. "But this may do the trick." He reached under his cloak and unsheathed the salmon scale dagger Stephan had given him. He extended his arm and pointed the dagger up towards the large crow perched in the tree. The short blade glinted in the starlight, adding a nice flair to his reveal.

To his delight, the crow had the sense to give a surprised squawk and jump a few branches higher.

Diego's teeth flashed in satisfaction. "So, Ol' Chancy, no singing. Or you'll be meeting this blade."

Ol' Chancy fluffed his feathers in irritation and turned his head to the side, an inky-black eye swimming in suspicion as it took in the finely forged steel pointed his way.

"Mighty interesting. Mighty interesting, indeed. Fine, Kitty. No lullaby. But I can't promise not to greet the sun with a little song when she rises," the crow said, looking to the east. "But really, I ain't here to annoy ya. Not entirely. Ol' Chauncy's got some wisdom to share."

Diego raised an eyebrow, skeptical. "Wisdom? From a crow?"

"Hey now, don't be so quick to judge. Crows be smart, ya know. We got more sense than most winged folk 'round here."

Diego sighed and paused his attempt at starting a fire. "Alright, what wisdom do you have to share, crow?"

The bird puffed out its chest, feeling rather pleased with itself. "Well, for starters, you're headed in the wrong direction."

Diego's ears pricked up, skepticism flaring. He had studied his maps for ages before leaving. "What do you mean?"

TO BE CONTINUED

Bibliography

Annie Hall. Directed by Woody Allen, United Artists, 1977.

Bakhtin, Mikhail. *The Dialogic Imagination: Four Essays*. Edited by Michael Holquist, University of Texas Press, 1981.

Barbie's Princess and the Pauper. Directed by William Lau, Mattel Entertainment, 2004.

Birdsong, Mia. *How We Show Up: Reclaiming Family, Friendship, and Community*. Hachette Go, 2020.

Bronte, Emily. *Wuthering Heights*. Thomas Cautley Newby, 1847.

Dederer, Claire. *Monsters: A Fan's Dilemma*. 1st ed., Penguin Random House, 2023.

Dederer, Claire. *Monsters: A Fan's Dilemma*. 1st ed., Penguin Random House, 2023, p. 174.

Dederer, Claire. *Monsters: A Fan's Dilemma*. 1st ed., Penguin Random House, 2023, p. 256.

Downey Jr., Robert, and Jude Law. *Sherlock Holmes*. Directed by Guy Ritchie, Warner Bros., 2009.

Estés, Clarissa Pinkola. *Women Who Run with the Wolves: Myths and Stories of the Wild Woman Archetype*. Ballantine Books, 1992.

Hemingway & Gellhorn. Directed by Philip Kaufman, HBO Films, 2012.

Holmes, Sir Arthur Conan. *The Adventures of Sherlock Holmes*. George Newnes Ltd, 1892.

Holmes, Sir Arthur Conan. *The Memoirs of Sherlock Holmes*. George Newnes Ltd, 1893.

Hugo, Victor. *The Hunchback of Notre-Dame*. Pierre-Jules Hetzel, 1831.

Jackson, Shirley. *Hangsaman*. Viking Press, 1951.

Jackson, Shirley. *The Lottery and Other Stories*. Farrar, Straus and Giroux, 1949.

Jackson, Shirley. *We Have Always Lived in the Castle*. Viking Press, 1962.

Kardashian, Kim. *The Kardashians*. E! Entertainment Television, 2022.

Kierkegaard, Søren. *Either/Or: A Fragment of Life*. Translated by Alastair Hannay, Penguin Classics, 1987.

Midnight in Paris. Directed by Woody Allen, Gravier Productions, 2011.

Piastrelli, Becca. *Root & Ritual: Timeless Ways to Connect with Land, Lineage, and Life*. Sounds True, 2021.

Reid, Ava. *Juniper & Thorn*. Harper Voyager, 2022.

Sherlock. Created by Steven Moffat and Mark Gatiss, BBC, 2010–2017.

Shirley. Directed by Josephine Decker, 2020.

Swift, Taylor. *1989 (Taylor's Version)*. Republic Records, 2023.

The Haunting of Hill House. Directed by Mike Flanagan, Netflix, 2018.

The Rocky Horror Picture Show. Directed by Jim Sharman, 20th Century Fox, 1975.

"People v. Levi Weeks, 1800." Historical Society of the New York Courts, 9 Mar. 2021, history.nycourts.gov/case/people-v-weeks/.

SAMANTHA NAGEL